FOREWORD

The collection of "Everything Will Be Okay" travel phrasebooks published by T&P Books is designed for people traveling abroad for tourism and business. The phrasebooks contain what matters most - the essentials for basic communication. This is an indispensable set of phrases to "survive" while abroad.

This phrasebook will help you in most cases where you need to ask something, get directions, find out how much something costs, etc. It can also resolve difficult communication situations where gestures just won't help.

This book contains a lot of phrases that have been grouped according to the most relevant topics. The edition also includes a small vocabulary that contains roughly 3,000 of the most frequently used words. Another section of the phrasebook provides a gastronomical dictionary that may help you order food at a restaurant or buy groceries at the store.

Take "Everything Will Be Okay" phrasebook with you on the road and you'll have an irreplaceable traveling companion who will help you find your way out of any situation and teach you to not fear speaking with foreigners.

TABLE OF CONTENTS

T&P Books Publishing

Travel phrasebooks collection
«Everything Will Be Okay!»

T&P Books Publishing

PHRASEBOOK

— SPANISH —

By Andrey Taranov

THE MOST IMPORTANT PHRASES

This phrasebook contains
the most important
phrases and questions
for basic communication
Everything you need
to survive overseas

Phrasebook + 3000-word dictionary

English-Spanish phrasebook & topical vocabulary

By Andrey Taranov

The collection of "Everything Will Be Okay" travel phrasebooks published by T&P Books is designed for people traveling abroad for tourism and business. The phrasebooks contain what matters most - the essentials for basic communication. This is an indispensable set of phrases to "survive" while abroad.

This book also includes a small topical vocabulary that contains roughly 3,000 of the most frequently used words. Another section of the phrasebook provides a gastronomical dictionary that may help you order food at a restaurant or buy groceries at the store.

T&P Books Publishing
www.tpbooks.com

ISBN: 978-1-78492-450-8

This book is also available in E-book formats.
Please visit www.tpbooks.com or the major online bookstores.

PRONUNCIATION

Letter	Spanish example	T&P phonetic alphabet	English example
a	grado	[a]	shorter than in ask
e	mermelada	[e]	elm, medal
i	física	[i]	shorter than in feet
o	tomo	[o]	pod, John
u	cubierta	[u]	book
b	baño, volar	[b]	baby, book
β	abeja	[β]	between b and v
d	dicho	[d]	day, doctor
ð	tirada	[ð]	weather, together
f	flauta	[f]	face, food
ʤ	azerbaidzhano	[ʤ]	joke, general
g	gorro	[g]	game, gold
	negro	[ɣ]	between [g] and [h]
j	botella	[j]	yes, New York
k	tabaco	[k]	clock, kiss
l	arqueólogo	[l]	lace, people
l	novela	lʲ	million
m	mosaico	[m]	magic, milk
	confitura	ɱ	nasal [m]
n	camino	[n]	name, normal
ŋ	blanco	[ŋ]	English, ring
p	zapatero	[p]	pencil, private
r	sabroso	[r]	rice, radio
s	asesor	[s]	city, boss
θ	lápiz	[θ]	month, tooth
t	estatua	[t]	tourist, trip
ʧ	lechuza	[ʧ]	church, French
v	Kiev	[v]	very, river
χ	dirigir	[χ]	as in Scots 'loch'
z	esgrima	[z]	zebra, please
ʃ	sheriff	[ʃ]	machine, shark
w	whisky	[w]	vase, winter

Letter	Spanish example	T&P phonetic alphabet	English example
'	[re'loχ]	'	primary stress
·	[aβre·'ʎatas]	·	interpunct

LIST OF ABBREVIATIONS

English abbreviations

ab.	-	about
adj	-	adjective
adv	-	adverb
anim.	-	animate
as adj	-	attributive noun used as adjective
e.g.	-	for example
etc.	-	et cetera
fam.	-	familiar
fem.	-	feminine
form.	-	formal
inanim.	-	inanimate
masc.	-	masculine
math	-	mathematics
mil.	-	military
n	-	noun
pl	-	plural
pron.	-	pronoun
sb	-	somebody
sing.	-	singular
sth	-	something
v aux	-	auxiliary verb
vi	-	intransitive verb
vi, vt	-	intransitive, transitive verb
vt	-	transitive verb

Spanish abbreviations

adj	-	adjective
adv	-	adverb
f	-	feminine noun
f pl	-	feminine plural
fam.	-	familiar
m	-	masculine noun
m pl	-	masculine plural
m, f	-	masculine, feminine
n	-	neuter

pl	-	plural
v aux	-	auxiliary verb
vi	-	intransitive verb
vi, vt	-	intransitive, transitive verb
vr	-	reflexive verb
vt	-	transitive verb

SPANISH PHRASEBOOK

This section contains important phrases that may come in handy in various real-life situations. The phrasebook will help you ask for directions, clarify a price, buy tickets, and order food at a restaurant

T&P Books Publishing

PHRASEBOOK CONTENTS

T&P Books Publishing

The bare minimum

Excuse me, …	**Perdone, …** [per'ðone, …]
Hello.	**Hola.** [ola]
Thank you.	**Gracias.** [graθjas]
Good bye.	**Adiós.** [a'ðjos]
Yes.	**Sí.** [si]
No.	**No.** [no]
I don't know.	**No lo sé.** [no lo 'se]
Where? | Where to? | When?	**¿Dónde? | ¿A dónde? | ¿Cuándo?** [donde? | a 'donde? | ku'ando?]

I need …	**Necesito …** [neθe'sito …]
I want …	**Quiero …** [kjero …]
Do you have …?	**¿Tiene …?** [tjene …?]
Is there a … here?	**¿Hay … por aquí?** [aj … por a'ki?]
May I …?	**¿Puedo …?** [pu'eðo …?]
…, please (polite request)	**…, por favor** […, por fa'βor]

I'm looking for …	**Busco …** [busko …]
the restroom	**el servicio** [elʲ ser'βiθjo]
an ATM	**un cajero** [un ka'χero]
a pharmacy (drugstore)	**una farmacia** [una far'maθja]
a hospital	**el hospital** [elʲ ospi'talʲ]
the police station	**la comisaría** [lʲa komisa'ria]
the subway	**el metro** [elʲ 'metro]

a taxi	**un taxi** [un 'taksi]
the train station	**la estación de tren** [lʲa esta'θjon de tren]

My name is ...	**Me llamo ...** [me 'jamo ...]
What's your name?	**¿Cómo se llama?** [komo se 'jama?]
Could you please help me?	**¿Puede ayudarme, por favor?** [pu'eðe aju'ðarme, por fa'βor?]
I've got a problem.	**Tengo un problema.** [tengo un pro'βlema]
I don't feel well.	**Me encuentro mal.** [me eŋku'entro malʲ]
Call an ambulance!	**¡Llame a la ambulancia!** [jame a la ambu'lanθja!]
May I make a call?	**¿Puedo llamar, por favor?** [pu'eðo ja'mar, por fa'βor?]

I'm sorry.	**Lo siento.** [lo 'sjento]
You're welcome.	**De nada.** [ðe 'naða]

I, me	**Yo** [jo]
you (inform.)	**tú** [tu]
he	**él** [elʲ]
she	**ella** [eja]
they (masc.)	**ellos** [ejos]
they (fem.)	**ellas** [ejas]
we	**nosotros** [no'sotros]
you (pl)	**ustedes | vosotros** [us'teðes | bo'sotros]
you (sg, form.)	**usted** [us'teð]

ENTRANCE	**ENTRADA** [en'traða]
EXIT	**SALIDA** [sa'liða]
OUT OF ORDER	**FUERA DE SERVICIO** [fu'era de ser'βiθjo]
CLOSED	**CERRADO** [θe'raðo]

OPEN	**ABIERTO** [a'βjerto]
FOR WOMEN	**PARA SEÑORAS** [para se'njoras]
FOR MEN	**PARA CABALLEROS** [para kaβa'jeros]

Questions

Where?	**¿Dónde?** [donde?]
Where to?	**¿A dónde?** [a 'donde?]
Where from?	**¿De dónde?** [de 'donde?]
Why?	**¿Por qué?** [por 'ke?]
For what reason?	**¿Con que razón?** [kon ke ra'θon?]
When?	**¿Cuándo?** [ku'ando?]
How long?	**¿Cuánto tiempo?** [ku'anto 'tjempo?]
At what time?	**¿A qué hora?** [a ke 'ora?]
How much?	**¿Cuánto?** [ku'anto?]
Do you have ...?	**¿Tiene ...?** [tjene ...?]
Where is ...?	**¿Dónde está ...?** [donde es'ta ...?]
What time is it?	**¿Qué hora es?** [ke 'ora es?]
May I make a call?	**¿Puedo llamar, por favor?** [pu'eðo ja'mar, por fa'βor?]
Who's there?	**¿Quién es?** [kjen es?]
Can I smoke here?	**¿Se puede fumar aquí?** [se pu'eðe fu'mar a'ki?]
May I ...?	**¿Puedo ...?** [pu'eðo ...?]

Needs

I'd like ...	**Quisiera ...** [ki'sjera ...]
I don't want ...	**No quiero ...** [no 'kjero ...]
I'm thirsty.	**Tengo sed.** [tengo seð]
I want to sleep.	**Tengo sueño.** [tengo su'enjo]

I want ...	**Quiero ...** [kjero ...]
to wash up	**lavarme** [l^{j}a'βarme]
to brush my teeth	**cepillarme los dientes** [θepi'jarme los 'djentes]
to rest a while	**descansar un poco** [deskan'sar un 'poko]
to change my clothes	**cambiarme de ropa** [kam'bjarme de 'ropa]

to go back to the hotel	**volver al hotel** [bol^j'βer al^j o'tel^j]
to buy ...	**comprar ...** [kom'prar ...]
to go to ...	**ir a ...** [ir a ...]
to visit ...	**visitar ...** [bisi'tar ...]
to meet with ...	**quedar con ...** [ke'ðar kon ...]
to make a call	**hacer una llamada** [a'θer un ja'maða]

I'm tired.	**Estoy cansado /cansada/.** [es'toj kan'saðo /kan'saða/]
We are tired.	**Estamos cansados /cansadas/.** [es'tamos kan'saðos /kan'saðas/]
I'm cold.	**Tengo frío.** [tengo 'frio]
I'm hot.	**Tengo calor.** [tengo ka'lor]
I'm OK.	**Estoy bien.** [es'toj bjen]

I need to make a call.	**Tengo que hacer una llamada.** [tengo ke a'θer 'una ja'maða]
I need to go to the restroom.	**Necesito ir al servicio.** [neθe'sito ir alʲ ser'βiθjo]
I have to go.	**Me tengo que ir.** [me 'tengo ke ir]
I have to go now.	**Me tengo que ir ahora.** [me 'tengo ke ir a'ora]

Asking for directions

Excuse me, ...	**Perdone, ...** [per'ðone, ...]
Where is ...?	**¿Dónde está ...?** [donde es'ta ...?]
Which way is ...?	**¿Por dónde está ...?** [por 'donde es'ta ...?]
Could you help me, please?	**¿Puede ayudarme, por favor?** [pu'eðe aju'ðarme, por fa'βor?]
I'm looking for ...	**Busco ...** [busko ...]
I'm looking for the exit.	**Busco la salida.** [busko lʲa sa'liða]
I'm going to ...	**Voy a ...** [boj a ...]
Am I going the right way to ...?	**¿Voy bien para ...?** [boj 'bjen 'para ...?]
Is it far?	**¿Está lejos?** [es'ta 'leχos?]
Can I get there on foot?	**¿Puedo llegar a pie?** [pu'eðo je'ɣar a pje?]
Can you show me on the map?	**¿Puede mostrarme en el mapa?** [pu'eðe mos'trarme en elʲ 'mapa?]
Show me where we are right now.	**Por favor muestreme dónde estamos.** [por fa'βor, mu'estreme 'donde es'tamos]
Here	**Aquí** [a'ki]
There	**Allí** [a'ji]
This way	**Por aquí** [por a'ki]
Turn right.	**Gire a la derecha.** [χire a lʲa de'retʃa]
Turn left.	**Gire a la izquierda.** [χire a lʲa iθ'kjerða]
first (second, third) turn	**la primera (segunda, tercera) calle** [lʲa pri'mera (se'ɣunda, ter'θera) 'kaje]
to the right	**a la derecha** [a lʲa de'retʃa]

to the left	**a la izquierda** [a lʲa iθ'kjerða]
Go straight ahead.	**Siga recto.** [siɣa 'rekto]

Signs

WELCOME!	**¡BIENVENIDO!** [bjembe'niðo!]
ENTRANCE	**ENTRADA** [en'traða]
EXIT	**SALIDA** [sa'liða]
PUSH	**EMPUJAR** [empu'χar]
PULL	**TIRAR** [ti'rar]
OPEN	**ABIERTO** [a'βjerto]
CLOSED	**CERRADO** [θe'raðo]
FOR WOMEN	**PARA SEÑORAS** [para se'njoras]
FOR MEN	**PARA CABALLEROS** [para kaβa'jeros]
GENTLEMEN, GENTS	**CABALLEROS** [kaβa'jeros]
WOMEN	**SEÑORAS** [se'njoras]
DISCOUNTS	**REBAJAS** [re'βaχas]
SALE	**VENTA** [benta]
FREE	**GRATIS** ['gratis]
NEW!	**¡NUEVO!** [nu'eβo!]
ATTENTION!	**ATENCIÓN!** [aten'θjon!]
NO VACANCIES	**COMPLETO** [kom'pleto]
RESERVED	**RESERVADO** [reser'βaðo]
ADMINISTRATION	**ADMINISTRACIÓN** [aðministra'θjon]
STAFF ONLY	**SÓLO PERSONAL AUTORIZADO** [solo perso'nal autori'θaðo]

BEWARE OF THE DOG!	**CUIDADO CON EL PERRO** [kui'ðaðo kon elʲ 'pero]
NO SMOKING!	**NO FUMAR** [no fu'mar]
DO NOT TOUCH!	**NO TOCAR** [no to'kar]
DANGEROUS	**PELIGROSO** [peli'ɣroso]
DANGER	**PELIGRO** [pe'liɣro]
HIGH VOLTAGE	**ALTA TENSIÓN** [alʲta ten'θjon]
NO SWIMMING!	**PROHIBIDO BAÑARSE** [proi'βiðo ba'njarse]

OUT OF ORDER	**FUERA DE SERVICIO** [fu'era de ser'βiθjo]
FLAMMABLE	**INFLAMABLE** [iɱfla'maβle]
FORBIDDEN	**PROHIBIDO** [proi'βiðo]
NO TRESPASSING!	**PROHIBIDO EL PASO** [proi'βiðo elʲ 'paso]
WET PAINT	**RECIÉN PINTADO** [re'θjen pin'taðo]

CLOSED FOR RENOVATIONS	**CERRADO POR RENOVACIÓN** [θe'raðo por renoβa'θjon]
WORKS AHEAD	**EN OBRAS** [en 'oβras]
DETOUR	**DESVÍO** [des'βio]

Transportation. General phrases

plane	**el avión** [elʲ a'βjon]
train	**el tren** [elʲ tren]
bus	**el bus** [elʲ bus]
ferry	**el ferry** [elʲ 'feri]
taxi	**el taxi** [elʲ 'taksi]
car	**el coche** [elʲ 'kotʃe]

---

schedule	**el horario** [elʲ o'rarjo]
Where can I see the schedule?	**¿Dónde puedo ver el horario?** [donde pu'eðo ber elʲ o'rarjo?]
workdays (weekdays)	**días laborables** [dias laβo'raβles]
weekends	**fines de semana** [fines de se'mana]
holidays	**días festivos** [dias fes'tiβos]

DEPARTURE	**SALIDA** [sa'liða]
ARRIVAL	**LLEGADA** [je'ɣaða]
DELAYED	**RETRASADO** [retra'saðo]
CANCELLED	**CANCELADO** [kanθe'lʲaðo]

---

next (train, etc.)	**siguiente** [si'ɣjente]
first	**primer** [pri'mer]
last	**último** [ulʲtimo]

When is the next ...?	**¿Cuándo pasa el siguiente ...?** [ku'ando 'pasa elʲ si'ɣjente ...?]
When is the first ...?	**¿Cuándo pasa el primer ...?** [ku'ando 'pasa elʲ pri'mer ...?]

When is the last ...?	**¿Cuándo pasa el último ...?** [ku'ando 'pasa el^{j} 'ul^{j}timo ...?]
transfer (change of trains, etc.)	**el trasbordo** [el^{j} tras'βorðo]
to make a transfer	**hacer un trasbordo** [a'θer un tras'βorðo]
Do I need to make a transfer?	**¿Tengo que hacer un trasbordo?** [tengo ke a'θer un tras'βorðo?]

Buying tickets

Where can I buy tickets?	**¿Dónde puedo comprar un billete?** [donde pu'eðo komp'rar un bi'jete?]
ticket	**el billete** [elʲ bi'jete]
to buy a ticket	**comprar un billete** [kom'prar un bi'jete]
ticket price	**precio del billete** [preθjo delʲ bi'jete]

Where to?	**¿Para dónde?** [para 'donde?]
To what station?	**¿A qué estación?** [a ke esta'θjon?]
I need ...	**Necesito ...** [neθe'sito ...]
one ticket	**un billete** [un bi'jete]
two tickets	**dos billetes** [dos bi'jetes]
three tickets	**tres billetes** [tres bi'jetes]

one-way	**sólo ida** [solo 'iða]
round-trip	**ida y vuelta** [iða i bu'elʲta]
first class	**en primera** [en pri'mera]
second class	**en segunda** [en se'ɣunda]

today	**hoy** [oj]
tomorrow	**mañana** [ma'njana]
the day after tomorrow	**pasado mañana** [pa'saðo ma'njana]
in the morning	**por la mañana** [por lʲa ma'njana]
in the afternoon	**por la tarde** [por lʲa 'tarðe]
in the evening	**por la noche** [por lʲa 'notʃe]

aisle seat	**asiento de pasillo** [a'sjento de pa'sijo]
window seat	**asiento de ventanilla** [a'sjento de benta'nija]
How much?	**¿Cuánto cuesta?** [ku'anto ku'esta?]
Can I pay by credit card?	**¿Puedo pagar con tarjeta?** [pu'eðo pa'ɣar kon tar'χeta?]

Bus

bus	**el autobús** [elʲ auto'βus]
intercity bus	**el autobús interurbano** [elʲ auto'βus interur'βano]
bus stop	**la parada de autobús** [lʲa pa'raða de auto'βus]
Where's the nearest bus stop?	**¿Dónde está la parada de autobuses más cercana?** [donde es'ta lʲa pa'raða de auto'βuses mas θer'kana?]
number (bus ~, etc.)	**número** [numero]
Which bus do I take to get to …?	**¿Qué autobús tengo que tomar para …?** [ke auto'βus 'tengo ke to'mar 'para …?]
Does this bus go to …?	**¿Este autobús va a …?** [este auto'βus 'ba a …?]
How frequent are the buses?	**¿Cada cuanto pasa el autobús?** [kaða ku'anto 'pasa elʲ auto'βus?]
every 15 minutes	**cada quince minutos** [kaða 'kinθe mi'nutos]
every half hour	**cada media hora** [kaða 'meðja 'ora]
every hour	**cada hora** [kaða 'ora]
several times a day	**varias veces al día** [barjas 'beθes alʲ 'dia]
… times a day	**… veces al día** [… 'beθes alʲ 'dia]
schedule	**el horario** [elʲ o'rarjo]
Where can I see the schedule?	**¿Dónde puedo ver el horario?** [donde pu'eðo ber elʲ o'rarjo?]
When is the next bus?	**¿Cuándo pasa el siguiente autobús?** [ku'ando 'pasa elʲ si'ɣjente auto'βus?]
When is the first bus?	**¿Cuándo pasa el primer autobús?** [ku'ando 'pasa elʲ pri'mer auto'βus?]
When is the last bus?	**¿Cuándo pasa el último autobús?** [ku'ando 'pasa elʲ 'ulʲtimo auto'βus?]

stop	**la parada** [lʲa pa'raða]
next stop	**la siguiente parada** [lʲa si'ɣjente pa'raða]
last stop (terminus)	**la última parada** [lʲa 'ulʲtima pa'raða]
Stop here, please.	**Pare aquí, por favor.** [pare a'ki, por fa'βor]
Excuse me, this is my stop.	**Perdone, esta es mi parada.** [per'ðone, 'esta es mi pa'raða]

Train

train	**el tren** [elʲ tren]
suburban train	**el tren de cercanías** [elʲ tren de θerka'nias]
long-distance train	**el tren de larga distancia** [elʲ tren de 'larɣa dis'tanθja]
train station	**la estación de tren** [lʲa esta'θjon de tren]
Excuse me, where is the exit to the platform?	**Perdone, ¿dónde está la salida al anden?** [per'ðone, 'donde es'ta lʲa sa'liða alʲ 'anden?]
Does this train go to ...?	**¿Este tren va a ...?** [este tren 'ba a ...?]
next train	**el siguiente tren** [elʲ si'ɣjente tren]
When is the next train?	**¿Cuándo pasa el siguiente tren?** [ku'ando 'pasa elʲ si'ɣjente tren?]
Where can I see the schedule?	**¿Dónde puedo ver el horario?** [donde pu'eðo ber elʲ o'rarjo?]
From which platform?	**¿De qué andén?** [ðe ke an'den?]
When does the train arrive in ...?	**¿Cuándo llega el tren a ...?** [ku'ando 'jeɣa elʲ tren a ...?]
Please help me.	**Ayudeme, por favor.** [a'juðeme, por fa'βor]
I'm looking for my seat.	**Busco mi asiento.** [busko mi a'sjento]
We're looking for our seats.	**Buscamos nuestros asientos.** [bus'kamos nu'estros a'sjentos]
My seat is taken.	**Mi asiento está ocupado.** [mi a'sjento es'ta oku'paðo]
Our seats are taken.	**Nuestros asientos están ocupados.** [nu'estros a'sjentos es'tan oku'paðos]
I'm sorry but this is my seat.	**Perdone, pero ese es mi asiento.** [per'ðone, 'pero 'ese es mi a'sjento]
Is this seat taken?	**¿Está libre?** [es'ta 'liβre?]
May I sit here?	**¿Puedo sentarme aquí?** [pu'eðo sen'tarme a'ki?]

On the train. Dialogue (No ticket)

Ticket, please.	**Su billete, por favor.** [su bi'jete, por fa'βor]
I don't have a ticket.	**No tengo billete.** [no 'tengo bi'jete]
I lost my ticket.	**He perdido mi billete.** [e per'ðiðo mi bi'jete]
I forgot my ticket at home.	**He olvidado mi billete en casa.** [e olʲβi'ðaðo mi bi'jete en 'kasa]
You can buy a ticket from me.	**Le puedo vender un billete.** [le pu'eðo ben'der un bi'jete]
You will also have to pay a fine.	**También deberá pagar una multa.** [tam'bjen deβe'ra pa'ɣar 'una 'mulʲta]
Okay.	**Vale.** ['bale]
Where are you going?	**¿Adónde va usted?** [a'ðonde ba us'te?]
I'm going to ...	**Voy a ...** [boj a ...]
How much? I don't understand.	**¿Cuánto es? No lo entiendo.** [ku'anto es? no lʲo en'tjendo]
Write it down, please.	**Escríbalo, por favor.** [es'kriβalo, por fa'βor]
Okay. Can I pay with a credit card?	**Vale. ¿Puedo pagar con tarjeta?** [bale. pu'eðo pa'ɣar kon tar'χeta?]
Yes, you can.	**Sí, puede.** [si, pu'eðe]
Here's your receipt.	**Aquí está su recibo.** [a'ki es'ta su re'θiβo]
Sorry about the fine.	**Disculpe por la multa.** [dis'kulʲpe por lʲa 'mulʲta]
That's okay. It was my fault.	**No pasa nada. Fue culpa mía.** [no 'pasa 'naða. 'fue 'kulʲpa 'mia]
Enjoy your trip.	**Disfrute su viaje.** [dis'frute su 'bjaχe]

Taxi

taxi	**taxi** ['taksi]
taxi driver	**taxista** [ta'ksista]
to catch a taxi	**coger un taxi** [ko'χer un 'taksi]
taxi stand	**parada de taxi** [pa'raða de 'taksi]
Where can I get a taxi?	**¿Dónde puedo coger un taxi?** [donde pu'eðo ko'χer un 'taksi?]

---

to call a taxi	**llamar a un taxi** [ja'mar a un 'taksi]
I need a taxi.	**Necesito un taxi.** [neθe'sito un 'taksi]
Right now.	**Ahora mismo.** [a'ora 'mismo]
What is your address (location)?	**¿Cuál es su dirección?** [ku'al^{j} es su direk'θjon?]
My address is ...	**Mi dirección es ...** [mi direk'θjon es ...]
Your destination?	**¿Cuál es el destino?** [ku'al^{j} es el^{j} des'tino?]
Excuse me, ...	**Perdone, ...** [per'ðone, ...]
Are you available?	**¿Está libre?** [es'ta 'liβre?]
How much is it to get to ...?	**¿Cuánto cuesta ir a ...?** [ku'anto ku'esta ir a ...?]
Do you know where it is?	**¿Sabe usted dónde está?** [saβe us'te 'donde es'ta?]

Airport, please.	**Al aeropuerto, por favor.** [al^{j} aeropu'erto, por fa'βor]
Stop here, please.	**Pare aquí, por favor.** [pare a'ki, por fa'βor]
It's not here.	**No es aquí.** [no es a'ki]
This is the wrong address.	**La dirección no es correcta.** [l^{j}a direk'θjon no es ko'rekta]
Turn left.	**Gire a la izquierda.** [χire a l^{j}a iθ'kjerða]
Turn right.	**Gire a la derecha.** [χire a l^{j}a de'reʧa]

How much do I owe you?	**¿Cuánto le debo?** [ku'anto le 'deβo?]
I'd like a receipt, please.	**¿Me da un recibo, por favor?** [me da un re'θiβo, por fa'βor?]
Keep the change.	**Quédese con el cambio.** [keðese kon el[j] 'kambjo]

Would you please wait for me?	**Espéreme, por favor.** [es'pereme, por fa'βor]
five minutes	**cinco minutos** [θiŋko mi'nutos]
ten minutes	**diez minutos** [ðjeθ mi'nutos]
fifteen minutes	**quince minutos** [kinθe mi'nutos]
twenty minutes	**veinte minutos** [bejnte mi'nutos]
half an hour	**media hora** [meðja 'ora]

Hotel

Hello. — **Hola.**
[ola]

My name is ... — **Me llamo ...**
[me 'jamo ...]

I have a reservation. — **Tengo una reserva.**
[tengo 'una re'serβa]

I need ... — **Necesito ...**
[neθe'sito ...]

a single room — **una habitación individual**
[una aβita'θjon indiβiðu'alʲ]

a double room — **una habitación doble**
[una aβita'θjon 'doβle]

How much is that? — **¿Cuánto cuesta?**
[ku'anto ku'esta?]

That's a bit expensive. — **Es un poco caro.**
[es um 'poko 'karo]

Do you have anything else? — **¿Tiene alguna más?**
[tjene alʲ'ɣuna mas?]

I'll take it. — **Me quedo.**
[me 'keðo]

I'll pay in cash. — **Pagaré en efectivo.**
[paɣa're en efek'tiβo]

I've got a problem. — **Tengo un problema.**
[tengo un pro'βlema]

My ... is broken. — **Mi ... no funciona.**
[mi ... no fuŋk'θjona]

My ... is out of order. — **Mi ... está fuera de servicio.**
[mi ... es'ta fu'era de ser'βiθjo]

TV — **televisión**
[teleβi'θjon]

air conditioner — **aire acondicionado**
[ajre akondiθjo'naðo]

tap — **grifo**
[grifo]

---

shower — **ducha**
[duʧa]

sink — **lavabo**
[lʲa'βaβo]

safe — **caja fuerte**
[kaχa fu'erte]

door lock	**cerradura** [θera'ðura]
electrical outlet	**enchufe** [en'ʧufe]
hairdryer	**secador de pelo** [seka'ðor de 'pelo]

I don't have …	**No tengo …** [no 'tengo …]
water	**agua** [aɣua]
light	**luz** [lʲuθ]
electricity	**electricidad** [elektriθi'ðað]

Can you give me …?	**¿Me puede dar …?** [me pu'eðe dar …?]
a towel	**una toalla** [una to'aja]
a blanket	**una sábana** [una 'saβana]
slippers	**chanclas** ['ʧaŋklas]
a robe	**un albornoz** [un alʲ'βornoθ]
shampoo	**champú** [ʧam'pu]
soap	**jabón** [χa'βon]

I'd like to change rooms.	**Quisiera cambiar de habitación.** [ki'sjera kam'bjar de aβita'θjon]
I can't find my key.	**No puedo encontrar mi llave.** [no pu'eðo eŋkon'trar mi 'jaβe]
Could you open my room, please?	**Por favor abra mi habitación.** [por fa'βor 'aβra mi aβita'θjon]
Who's there?	**¿Quién es?** [kjen es?]
Come in!	**¡Entre!** [entre!]
Just a minute!	**¡Un momento!** [un mo'mento!]
Not right now, please.	**Ahora no, por favor.** [a'ora no, por fa'βor]

Come to my room, please.	**Venga a mi habitación, por favor.** [benga a mi aβita'θjon, por fa'βor]
I'd like to order food service.	**Quisiera hacer un pedido.** [ki'sjera a'θer un pe'ðiðo]
My room number is …	**Mi número de habitación es …** [min 'numero de aβita'θjon es …]

I'm leaving ...	**Me voy ...** [me boj ...]
We're leaving ...	**Nos vamos ...** [nos 'bamos ...]
right now	**Ahora mismo** [a'ora 'mismo]
this afternoon	**esta tarde** [esta 'tarðe]
tonight	**esta noche** [esta 'notʃe]
tomorrow	**mañana** [ma'njana]
tomorrow morning	**mañana por la mañana** [ma'njana por lʲa ma'njana]
tomorrow evening	**mañana por la noche** [ma'njana por lʲa 'notʃe]
the day after tomorrow	**pasado mañana** [pa'saðo ma'njana]

I'd like to pay.	**Quisiera pagar la cuenta.** [ki'sjera pa'ɣar la ku'enta]
Everything was wonderful.	**Todo ha estado estupendo.** [toðo a es'taðo estu'pendo]
Where can I get a taxi?	**¿Dónde puedo coger un taxi?** [donde pu'eðo ko'χer un 'taksi?]
Would you call a taxi for me, please?	**¿Puede llamarme un taxi, por favor?** [pu'eðe ja'marme un 'taksi, por fa'βor?]

Restaurant

Can I look at the menu, please?	**¿Puedo ver el menú, por favor?** [pu'eðo ber el^{j} me'nu, por fa'βor?]
Table for one.	**Mesa para uno.** [mesa 'para 'uno]
There are two (three, four) of us.	**Somos dos (tres, cuatro).** [somos dos (tres, ku'atro)]
Smoking	**Para fumadores** [para fuma'ðores]
No smoking	**Para no fumadores** [para no fuma'ðores]
Excuse me! (addressing a waiter)	**¡Por favor!** [por fa'βor!]
menu	**la carta, el menú** [l^{j}a 'karta, el^{j} me'nu]
wine list	**la carta de vinos** [l^{j}a 'karta de 'binos]
The menu, please.	**La carta, por favor.** [l^{j}a 'karta, por fa'βor]
Are you ready to order?	**¿Está listo /lista/ para pedir?** [es'ta 'listo /'lista/ 'para pe'ðir?]
What will you have?	**¿Qué quieren pedir?** [ke 'kjeren pe'ðir?]
I'll have ...	**Yo quiero ...** [jo 'kjero ...]
I'm a vegetarian.	**Soy vegetariano /vegetariana/.** [soj beχeta'rjano /beχeta'rjana/]
meat	**carne** [karne]
fish	**pescado** [pes'kaðo]
vegetables	**verduras** [ber'ðuras]
Do you have vegetarian dishes?	**¿Tiene platos para vegetarianos?** [tjene 'platos 'para beχeta'rjanos?]
I don't eat pork.	**No como cerdo.** [no 'komo 'θerðo]
Band-Aid	**Él /Ella/ no come carne.** [el^{j} /'eja/ no 'kome 'karne]
I am allergic to ...	**Soy alérgico /alérgica/ a ...** [soj a'lerχiko /a'lerχika/ a ...]

Would you please bring me ... — **¿Me puede traer ..., por favor?**
[me pu'eðe tra'er, ... por fa'βor?]

salt | pepper | sugar — **sal | pimienta | azúcar**
[salʲ | pi'mjenta | a'θukar]

coffee | tea | dessert — **café | té | postre**
[ka'fe | te | 'postre]

water | sparkling | plain — **agua | con gas | sin gas**
[aɣua | kon gas | sin gas]

a spoon | fork | knife — **una cuchara | un tenedor | un cuchillo**
[una ku'ʧara | un tene'ðor | un ku'ʧijo]

a plate | napkin — **un plato | una servilleta**
[un 'plato | una serβi'jeta]

Enjoy your meal! — **¡Buen provecho!**
[bu'en pro'βeʧo!]

One more, please. — **Uno más, por favor.**
[uno mas, por fa'βor]

It was very delicious. — **Estaba delicioso.**
[es'taβa deli'θjoso]

---

check | change | tip — **la cuenta | el cambio | la propina**
[lʲa ku'enta | elʲ 'kambio | lʲa pro'pina]

Check, please.
(Could I have the check, please?) — **La cuenta, por favor.**
[lʲa ku'enta, por fa'βor]

Can I pay by credit card? — **¿Puedo pagar con tarjeta?**
[pu'eðo pa'ɣar kon tar'χeta?]

I'm sorry, there's a mistake here. — **Perdone, aquí hay un error.**
[per'ðone, a'ki aj un e'ror]

Shopping

Can I help you? — **¿Puedo ayudarle?**
[pu'eðo aju'ðarle?]

Do you have ...? — **¿Tiene ...?**
[tjene ...?]

I'm looking for ... — **Busco ...**
[busko ...]

I need ... — **Necesito ...**
[neθe'sito ...]

I'm just looking. — **Sólo estoy mirando.**
[solo es'toj mi'rando]

We're just looking. — **Sólo estamos mirando.**
[solo es'tamos mi'rando]

I'll come back later. — **Volveré más tarde.**
[bolʲβe're mas 'tarðe]

We'll come back later. — **Volveremos más tarde.**
[bolʲβe'remos mas 'tarðe]

discounts | sale — **descuentos | oferta**
[desku'entos | o'ferta]

Would you please show me ... — **Por favor, enséñeme ...**
[por fa'βor, en'senjeme ...]

Would you please give me ... — **¿Me puede dar ..., por favor?**
[me pu'eðe dar, ... por fa'βor?]

Can I try it on? — **¿Puedo probarmelo?**
[pueðo pro'βarmelo?]

Excuse me, where's the fitting room? — **Perdone, ¿dónde están los probadores?**
[per'ðone, 'donde es'tan los proβa'ðores?]

Which color would you like? — **¿Qué color le gustaría?**
[ke ko'lor le gusta'ria?]

size | length — **la talla | el largo**
[lʲa 'taja | elʲ 'lʲarɣo]

How does it fit? — **¿Cómo le queda?**
[komo le 'keða?]

How much is it? — **¿Cuánto cuesta esto?**
[ku'anto ku'esta 'esto?]

That's too expensive. — **Es muy caro.**
[es muj 'karo]

I'll take it. — **Me lo llevo.**
[me lo 'jeβo]

Excuse me, where do I pay? — **Perdone, ¿dónde está la caja?**
[per'ðone, 'donde es'ta lʲa 'kaχa?]

Will you pay in cash or credit card?	**¿Pagará en efectivo o con tarjeta?** [paɣa'ra en efek'tiβo o kon tar'χeta?]
In cash | with credit card	**en efectivo | con tarjeta** [en efek'tiβo | kon tar'χeta]

Do you want the receipt?	**¿Quiere el recibo?** [kjere el[j] re'θiβo?]
Yes, please.	**Sí, por favor.** [si, por fa'βor]
No, it's OK.	**No, gracias.** [no, 'graθjas]
Thank you. Have a nice day!	**Gracias. ¡Que tenga un buen día!** [graθjas. ke 'tenga un bu'en 'dia!]

In town

Excuse me, ...	**Perdone, por favor.** [per'ðone, por fa'βor]
I'm looking for ...	**Busco ...** [busko ...]
the subway	**el metro** [elʲ 'metro]
my hotel	**mi hotel** [mi o'telʲ]
the movie theater	**el cine** [elʲ 'θine]
a taxi stand	**una parada de taxi** [una pa'raða de 'taksi]

---

an ATM	**un cajero** [un ka'χero]
a foreign exchange office	**una oficina de cambio** [una ofi'θina de 'kambjo]
an internet café	**un cibercafé** [un 'θiβer·ka'fe]
... street	**la calle ...** [lʲa 'kaje ...]
this place	**este lugar** [este lʲu'ɣar]

Do you know where ... is?	**¿Sabe usted dónde está ...?** [saβe us'te 'donde es'ta ...?]
Which street is this?	**¿Cómo se llama esta calle?** [komo se 'jama 'esta 'kalʲe?]
Show me where we are right now.	**Muestreme dónde estamos ahora.** [mu'estreme 'donde es'tamos a'ora]
Can I get there on foot?	**¿Puedo llegar a pie?** [pu'eðo je'ɣar a pje?]
Do you have a map of the city?	**¿Tiene un mapa de la ciudad?** [tjene un 'mapa de lʲa θju'ðað?]

How much is a ticket to get in?	**¿Cuánto cuesta la entrada?** [ku'anto ku'esta lʲa en'traða?]
Can I take pictures here?	**¿Se pueden hacer fotos aquí?** [se pu'eðen a'θer 'fotos a'ki?]
Are you open?	**¿Está abierto?** [es'ta a'βjerto?]

When do you open? — **¿A qué hora abren?**
[a ke 'ora 'aβren?]

When do you close? — **¿A qué hora cierran?**
[a ke 'ora 'θjeran?]

Money

money	**dinero** [ði'nero]
cash	**efectivo** [efek'tiβo]
paper money	**billetes** [bi'jetes]
loose change	**monedas** [mo'neðas]
check | change | tip	**la cuenta | el cambio | la propina** [lʲa ku'enta | elʲ 'kambio | lʲa pro'pina]

credit card	**la tarjeta de crédito** [lʲa tar'χeta de 'kreðito]
wallet	**la cartera** [lʲa kar'tera]
to buy	**comprar** [kom'prar]
to pay	**pagar** [pa'ɣar]
fine	**la multa** [lʲa 'mulʲta]
free	**gratis** ['gratis]

Where can I buy ...?	**¿Dónde puedo comprar ...?** [donde pu'eðo kom'prar ...?]
Is the bank open now?	**¿Está el banco abierto ahora?** [es'ta elʲ 'baŋko a'βjerta a'ora?]
When does it open?	**¿A qué hora abre?** [a ke 'ora 'aβre?]
When does it close?	**¿A qué hora cierra?** [a ke 'ora 'θjera?]

How much?	**¿Cuánto cuesta?** [ku'anto ku'esta?]
How much is this?	**¿Cuánto cuesta esto?** [ku'anto ku'esta 'esto?]
That's too expensive.	**Es muy caro.** [es muj 'karo]

Excuse me, where do I pay?	**Perdone, ¿dónde está la caja?** [per'ðone, 'donde es'ta lʲa 'kaχa?]
Check, please.	**La cuenta, por favor.** [lʲa ku'enta, por fa'βor]

Can I pay by credit card?	**¿Puedo pagar con tarjeta?** [pu'eðo pa'ɣar kon tar'χeta?]
Is there an ATM here?	**¿Hay un cajero por aquí?** [aj un ka'χero por a'ki?]
I'm looking for an ATM.	**Busco un cajero automático.** [nese'sito un ka'χero auto'matiko]

I'm looking for a foreign exchange office.	**Busco una oficina de cambio.** [busko 'una ofi'θina de 'kambjo]
I'd like to change ...	**Quisiera cambiar ...** [ki'sjera kam'bjar ...]
What is the exchange rate?	**¿Cuál es el tipo de cambio?** [ku'alʲ es elʲ 'tipo de 'kambjo?]
Do you need my passport?	**¿Necesita mi pasaporte?** [neθe'sita mi pasa'porte?]

Time

What time is it?	**¿Qué hora es?** [ke 'ora es?]
When?	**¿Cuándo?** [ku'ando?]
At what time?	**¿A qué hora?** [a ke 'ora?]
now | later | after ...	**ahora | luego | después de ...** [a'ora | lʲu'eɣo | despu'es de ...]
one o'clock	**la una** [lʲa 'una]
one fifteen	**la una y cuarto** [lʲa 'una i ku'arto]
one thirty	**la una y medio** [lʲa 'una i 'meðjo]
one forty-five	**las dos menos cuarto** [lʲa dos 'menos ku'arto]
one | two | three	**una | dos | tres** [una | dos | tres]
four | five | six	**cuatro | cinco | seis** [ku'atro | 'θiŋko | 'seis]
seven | eight | nine	**siete | ocho | nueve** [sjete | 'oʧo | nu'eβe]
ten | eleven | twelve	**diez | once | doce** [djeθ | 'onθe | 'doθe]
in ...	**en ...** [en ...]
five minutes	**cinco minutos** [θiŋko mi'nutos]
ten minutes	**diez minutos** [ðjeθ mi'nutos]
fifteen minutes	**quince minutos** [kinθe mi'nutos]
twenty minutes	**veinte minutos** [bejnte mi'nutos]
half an hour	**media hora** [meðja 'ora]
an hour	**una hora** [una 'ora]

in the morning	**por la mañana** [por lʲa ma'njana]
early in the morning	**por la mañana temprano** [por lʲa ma'njana tem'prano]
this morning	**esta mañana** [esta ma'njana]
tomorrow morning	**mañana por la mañana** [ma'njana por lʲa ma'njana]

in the middle of the day	**al mediodía** [alʲ meðjo'ðia]
in the afternoon	**por la tarde** [por lʲa 'tarðe]
in the evening	**por la noche** [por lʲa 'notʃe]
tonight	**esta noche** [esta 'notʃe]

at night	**por la noche** [por lʲa 'notʃe]
yesterday	**ayer** [a'jer]
today	**hoy** [oj]
tomorrow	**mañana** [ma'njana]
the day after tomorrow	**pasado mañana** [pa'saðo ma'njana]

What day is it today?	**¿Qué día es hoy?** [ke 'dia es oj?]
It's ...	**Es ...** [es ...]
Monday	**lunes** [lʲunes]
Tuesday	**martes** [martes]
Wednesday	**miércoles** [mjerkoles]

Thursday	**jueves** [χu'eβes]
Friday	**viernes** [bjernes]
Saturday	**sábado** [saβaðo]
Sunday	**domingo** [do'mingo]

Greetings. Introductions

Hello.	**Hola.** [ola]
Pleased to meet you.	**Encantado /Encantada/ de conocerle.** [eŋkan'taðo /eŋkan'taða/ de kono'θerle]
Me too.	**Yo también.** [jo tam'bjen]
I'd like you to meet ...	**Le presento a ...** [le pre'sento a ...]
Nice to meet you.	**Encantado /Encantada/.** [eŋkan'taðo /eŋkan'taða/]

How are you?	**¿Cómo está?** [komo es'ta?]
My name is ...	**Me llamo ...** [me 'jamo ...]
His name is ...	**Se llama ...** [se 'jama ...]
Her name is ...	**Se llama ...** [se 'jama ...]
What's your name?	**¿Cómo se llama?** [komo se 'jama?]
What's his name?	**¿Cómo se llama?** [komo se 'jama?]
What's her name?	**¿Cómo se llama?** [komo se 'jama?]
What's your last name?	**¿Cuál es su apellido?** [ku'alʲ es su ape'jiðo?]
You can call me ...	**Puede llamarme ...** [pu'eðo ja'marme ...]
Where are you from?	**¿De dónde es usted?** [de 'donde es us'te?]
I'm from ...	**Yo soy de ....** [jo soj de ...]
What do you do for a living?	**¿A qué se dedica?** [a ke se de'ðika?]

Who is this?	**¿Quién es?** [kjen es?]
Who is he?	**¿Quién es él?** [kjen es elʲ?]
Who is she?	**¿Quién es ella?** [kjen es 'eja?]
Who are they?	**¿Quiénes son?** [kjenes son?]

This is ...	**Este /Esta/ es ...** [este /'esta/ es ...]
my friend (masc.)	**mi amigo** [mi a'miɣo]
my friend (fem.)	**mi amiga** [mi a'miɣa]
my husband	**mi marido** [mi ma'riðo]
my wife	**mi mujer** [mi mu'χer]

---

my father	**mi padre** [mi 'paðre]
my mother	**mi madre** [mi 'maðre]
my brother	**mi hermano** [mi er'mano]
my sister	**mi hermana** [mi er'mana]
my son	**mi hijo** [mi 'iχo]
my daughter	**mi hija** [mi 'iχa]

This is our son.	**Este es nuestro hijo.** [este es nu'estro 'iχo]
This is our daughter.	**Esta es nuestra hija.** [esta es nu'estra 'iχa]
These are my children.	**Estos son mis hijos.** [estos son mis 'iχos]
These are our children.	**Estos son nuestros hijos.** [estos son nu'estros 'iχos]

Farewells

Good bye!	**¡Adiós!** [a'ðjos!]
Bye! (inform.)	**¡Chau!** ['ʧau!]
See you tomorrow.	**Hasta mañana.** [asta ma'njana]
See you soon.	**Hasta pronto.** [asta 'pronto]
See you at seven.	**Te veo a las siete.** [te 'beo a las 'sjete]
Have fun!	**¡Que se diviertan!** [ke se di'βjertan!]
Talk to you later.	**Hablamos más tarde.** [a'βlamos mas 'tarðe]
Have a nice weekend.	**Que tengas un buen fin de semana.** [ke 'tengas un bu'en fin de se'mana]
Good night.	**Buenas noches.** [bu'enas 'noʧes]
It's time for me to go.	**Es hora de irme.** [es 'ora de 'irme]
I have to go.	**Tengo que irme.** [tengo ke 'irme]
I will be right back.	**Ahora vuelvo.** [a'ora bu'elʲβo]
It's late.	**Es tarde.** [es 'tarðe]
I have to get up early.	**Tengo que levantarme temprano.** [tengo ke leβan'tarme tem'prano]
I'm leaving tomorrow.	**Me voy mañana.** [me boj ma'njana]
We're leaving tomorrow.	**Nos vamos mañana.** [nos 'bamos ma'njana]
Have a nice trip!	**¡Que tenga un buen viaje!** [ke 'tenga un bu'en 'bjaχe!]
It was nice meeting you.	**Ha sido un placer.** [a 'siðo um pla'θer]
It was nice talking to you.	**Fue un placer hablar con usted.** [fue un pla'θer a'βlar kon us'te]
Thanks for everything.	**Gracias por todo.** [graθjas por 'toðo]

I had a very good time. | **Lo he pasado muy bien.**
[lo e pa'saðo muj bjen]

We had a very good time. | **Lo pasamos muy bien.**
[lo pa'samos muj bjen]

It was really great. | **Fue genial.**
[fue χe'njal^j]

I'm going to miss you. | **Le voy a echar de menos.**
[le boj a e'ʧar de 'menos]

We're going to miss you. | **Le vamos a echar de menos.**
[le 'bamos a e'ʧar de 'menos]

Good luck! | **¡Suerte!**
[su'erte!]

Say hi to ... | **Saludos a ...**
[sal^ju'ðos a ...]

Foreign language

I don't understand.	**No entiendo.** [no en'tjendo]
Write it down, please.	**Escríbalo, por favor.** [es'kriβalo, por fa'βor]
Do you speak ...?	**¿Habla usted ...?** [aβla us'te ...?]
I speak a little bit of ...	**Hablo un poco de ...** [aβlo um 'poko de ...]
English	**inglés** [in'gles]
Turkish	**turco** [turko]
Arabic	**árabe** [araβe]
French	**francés** [fran'θes]
German	**alemán** [ale'man]
Italian	**italiano** [ita'ljano]
Spanish	**español** [espa'njol]
Portuguese	**portugués** [portu'ɣes]
Chinese	**chino** [ʧino]
Japanese	**japonés** [χapo'nes]
Can you repeat that, please.	**¿Puede repetirlo, por favor?** [pu'eðe repe'tirlo, por fa'βor?]
I understand.	**Lo entiendo.** [lo en'tjendo]
I don't understand.	**No entiendo.** [no en'tjendo]
Please speak more slowly.	**Hable más despacio, por favor.** [aβle mas des'paθjo, por fa'βor]
Is that correct? (Am I saying it right?)	**¿Está bien?** [es'ta bjen?]
What is this? (What does this mean?)	**¿Qué es esto?** [ke es 'esto?]

Apologies

Excuse me, please.	**Perdone, por favor.** [per'ðone, por fa'βor]
I'm sorry.	**Lo siento.** [lo 'sjento]
I'm really sorry.	**Lo siento mucho.** [lo 'sjento 'mutʃo]
Sorry, it's my fault.	**Perdón, fue culpa mía.** [per'ðon, 'fue 'kulʲpa 'mia]
My mistake.	**Culpa mía.** [kulʲpa 'mia]

May I ...?	**¿Puedo ...?** [pu'eðo ...?]
Do you mind if I ...?	**¿Le molesta si ...?** [le mo'lesta si ...?]
It's OK.	**¡No hay problema!** [no aj pro'βlema]
It's all right.	**Todo está bien.** [toðo es'ta bjen]
Don't worry about it.	**No se preocupe.** [no se preo'kupe]

Agreement

Yes.	**Sí.** [si]
Yes, sure.	**Sí, claro.** [si, 'klaro]
OK (Good!)	**Bien.** [bjen]
Very well.	**Muy bien.** [muj bjen]
Certainly!	**¡Claro que sí!** [klaro ke 'si!]
I agree.	**Estoy de acuerdo.** [es'toj de aku'erðo]
That's correct.	**Es verdad.** [es ber'ðað]
That's right.	**Es correcto.** [es ko'rekto]
You're right.	**Tiene razón.** [tjene ra'θon]
I don't mind.	**No me molesta.** [no me mo'lesta]
Absolutely right.	**Es completamente cierto.** [es kompleta'mente 'θjerto]
It's possible.	**Es posible.** [es po'siβle]
That's a good idea.	**Es una buena idea.** [es 'una bu'ena i'ðea]
I can't say no.	**No puedo decir que no.** [no pu'eðo deθ'ir ke no]
I'd be happy to.	**Estaré encantado /encantada/.** [esta're eŋkan'taðo /eŋkan'taða/]
With pleasure.	**Será un placer.** [se'ra un pla'θer]

Refusal. Expressing doubt

No.	**No.** [no]
Certainly not.	**Claro que no.** [klʲaro ke no]
I don't agree.	**No estoy de acuerdo.** [no es'toj de aku'erðo]
I don't think so.	**No lo creo.** [no lo 'kreo]
It's not true.	**No es verdad.** [no es ber'ðað]
You are wrong.	**No tiene razón.** [no 'tjene ra'θon]
I think you are wrong.	**Creo que no tiene razón.** [kreo ke no 'tjene ra'θon]
I'm not sure.	**No estoy seguro /segura/.** [no es'toj se'ɣuro /se'ɣura/]
It's impossible.	**No es posible.** [no es po'siβle]
Nothing of the kind (sort)!	**¡Nada de eso!** [naða de 'eso!]
The exact opposite.	**Justo lo contrario.** [χusto lo kon'trarjo!]
I'm against it.	**Estoy en contra.** [es'toj en 'kontra]
I don't care.	**No me importa.** [no me im'porta]
I have no idea.	**No tengo ni idea.** [no 'tengo ni i'ðea]
I doubt it.	**Dudo que sea así.** [duðo ke 'sea a'si]
Sorry, I can't.	**Lo siento, no puedo.** [lo 'sjento, no pu'eðo]
Sorry, I don't want to.	**Lo siento, no quiero.** [lo 'sjento, no 'kjero]
Thank you, but I don't need this.	**Gracias, pero no lo necesito.** [graθjas, 'pero no lo neθe'sito]
It's getting late.	**Ya es tarde.** [ja es 'tarðe]

I have to get up early.	**Tengo que levantarme temprano.** [tengo ke leβan'tarme tem'prano]
I don't feel well.	**Me encuentro mal.** [me eŋku'entro malʲ]

Expressing gratitude

Thank you.	**Gracias.** [graθjas]
Thank you very much.	**Muchas gracias.** [muʧas 'graθjas]
I really appreciate it.	**De verdad lo aprecio.** [ðe ber'ðað lo a'preθjo]
I'm really grateful to you.	**Se lo agradezco.** [se lo aɣra'ðeθko]
We are really grateful to you.	**Se lo agradecemos.** [se lo aɣraðe'θemos]
Thank you for your time.	**Gracias por su tiempo.** [graθjas por su 'tjempo]
Thanks for everything.	**Gracias por todo.** [graθjas por 'toðo]
Thank you for ...	**Gracias por ...** [graθjas por ...]
your help	**su ayuda** [su a'juða]
a nice time	**tan agradable momento** [tan aɣra'ðaβle mo'mento]
a wonderful meal	**una comida estupenda** [una ko'miða estu'penda]
a pleasant evening	**una velada tan agradable** [una be'laða tan aɣra'ðaβle]
a wonderful day	**un día maravilloso** [un 'dia maraβi'joso]
an amazing journey	**un viaje increíble** [un 'bjaχe iŋkre'iβle]
Don't mention it.	**No hay de qué.** [no aj de 'ke]
You are welcome.	**De nada.** [ðe 'naða]
Any time.	**Siempre a su disposición.** [sjempre a su dispozi'θjon]
My pleasure.	**Encantado /Encantada/ de ayudarle.** [eŋkan'taðo /eŋkan'taða/ de aju'ðarle]
Forget it.	**No hay de qué.** [no aj de 'ke]
Don't worry about it.	**No tiene importancia.** [no 'tjene impor'tanθja]

Congratulations. Best wishes

Congratulations!	**¡Felicidades!** [feliθi'ðaðes!]
Happy birthday!	**¡Feliz Cumpleaños!** [fe'liθ kumple'anjos!]
Merry Christmas!	**¡Feliz Navidad!** [fe'liθ naβi'ðað!]
Happy New Year!	**¡Feliz Año Nuevo!** [fe'liθ 'anjo nu'eβo!]
Happy Easter!	**¡Felices Pascuas!** [fe'liθes 'paskuas!]
Happy Hanukkah!	**¡Feliz Janucá!** [fe'liθ χanu'ka!]
I'd like to propose a toast.	**Quiero brindar.** [kjero brin'dar]
Cheers!	**¡Salud!** [sa'lʲuð]
Let's drink to ...!	**¡Brindemos por ...!** [brin'demos por ...!]
To our success!	**¡A nuestro éxito!** [a nu'estro 'eksito!]
To your success!	**¡A su éxito!** [a su 'eksito!]
Good luck!	**¡Suerte!** [su'erte!]
Have a nice day!	**¡Que tenga un buen día!** [ke 'tenga un bu'en 'dia!]
Have a good holiday!	**¡Que tenga unas buenas vacaciones!** [ke 'tengas 'unas bu'enas baka'θjones!]
Have a safe journey!	**¡Que tenga un buen viaje!** [ke 'tenga un bu'en 'bjaχe!]
I hope you get better soon!	**¡Espero que se recupere pronto!** [es'pero ke se reku'pere 'pronto!]

Socializing

Why are you sad?	**¿Por qué está triste?** [por 'ke es'ta 'triste?]
Smile! Cheer up!	**¡Sonría! ¡Anímese!** [son'ria! a'nimese!]
Are you free tonight?	**¿Está libre esta noche?** [es'ta 'liβre 'esta 'notʃe?]
May I offer you a drink?	**¿Puedo ofrecerle algo de beber?** [pu'eðo ofre'θerle 'alʲɣo de be'βer?]
Would you like to dance?	**¿Querría bailar conmigo?** [ker'ia baj'lar kon'miɣo?]
Let's go to the movies.	**Vamos a ir al cine.** [bamos a ir alʲ θ'ine]
May I invite you to ...?	**¿Puedo invitarle a ...?** [pu'eðo imbi'tarle a ...?]
a restaurant	**un restaurante** [un restau'rante]
the movies	**el cine** [elʲ 'θine]
the theater	**el teatro** [elʲ te'atro]
go for a walk	**dar una vuelta** [ðar 'una bu'elʲta]
At what time?	**¿A qué hora?** [a ke 'ora?]
tonight	**esta noche** [esta 'notʃe]
at six	**a las seis** [a las 'seis]
at seven	**a las siete** [a las 'sjete]
at eight	**a las ocho** [a las 'otʃo]
at nine	**a las nueve** [a las nu'eβe]
Do you like it here?	**¿Le gusta este lugar?** [le 'gusta 'este lʲu'ɣar?]
Are you here with someone?	**¿Está aquí con alguien?** [es'ta a'ki kon 'alʲɣjen?]
I'm with my friend.	**Estoy con mi amigo /amiga/.** [es'toj kon mi a'miɣo /a'miɣa/]

I'm with my friends.	**Estoy con amigos.** [es'toj kon a'miɣos]
No, I'm alone.	**No, estoy solo /sola/.** [no, es'toj 'solo /'sola/]

Do you have a boyfriend?	**¿Tienes novio?** [tjenes 'noβjo?]
I have a boyfriend.	**Tengo novio.** [tengo 'noβjo]
Do you have a girlfriend?	**¿Tienes novia?** [tjenes 'noβja?]
I have a girlfriend.	**Tengo novia.** [tengo 'noβja]

Can I see you again?	**¿Te puedo volver a ver?** [te pu'eðo bolʲβ'er a ber?]
Can I call you?	**¿Te puedo llamar?** [te pu'eðo ja'mar?]
Call me. (Give me a call.)	**Llámame.** [jamame]
What's your number?	**¿Cuál es tu número?** [ku'alʲ es tu 'numero?]
I miss you.	**Te echo de menos.** [te 'eʧo de 'menos]

You have a beautiful name.	**¡Qué nombre tan bonito!** [ke 'nombre tan bo'nito]
I love you.	**Te quiero.** [te 'kjero]
Will you marry me?	**¿Te casarías conmigo?** [te kasa'rias kon'miɣo?]
You're kidding!	**¡Está de broma!** [es'ta de 'broma!]
I'm just kidding.	**Sólo estoy bromeando.** [solo es'toj brome'ando]

Are you serious?	**¿En serio?** [en 'serjo?]
I'm serious.	**Lo digo en serio.** [lo 'diɣo en 'serjo]
Really?!	**¿De verdad?** [ðe ber'ðað?]
It's unbelievable!	**¡Es increíble!** [es iŋkre'iβle!]
I don't believe you.	**No le creo.** [no le 'kreo]
I can't.	**No puedo.** [no pu'eðo]
I don't know.	**No lo sé.** [no lo 'se]
I don't understand you.	**No le entiendo.** [no le en'tjendo]

Please go away.	**Váyase, por favor.** [bajase, por fa'βor]
Leave me alone!	**¡Déjeme en paz!** [ðeχeme en paθ!]

I can't stand him.	**Es inaguantable.** [es inaɣuan'taβle]
You are disgusting!	**¡Es un asqueroso!** [es un aske'roso!]
I'll call the police!	**¡Llamaré a la policía!** [jama're a lʲa poli'sia!]

Sharing impressions. Emotions

I like it.	**Me gusta.** [me 'gusta]
Very nice.	**Muy lindo.** [muj 'lindo]
That's great!	**¡Es genial!** [es χe'njalʲ!]
It's not bad.	**No está mal.** [no es'ta malʲ]
I don't like it.	**No me gusta.** [no me 'gusta]
It's not good.	**No está bien.** [no es'ta bjen]
It's bad.	**Está mal.** [es'ta malʲ]
It's very bad.	**Está muy mal.** [es'ta muj malʲ]
It's disgusting.	**¡Qué asco!** [ke 'asko]
I'm happy.	**Estoy feliz.** [es'toj fe'liθ]
I'm content.	**Estoy contento /contenta/.** [es'toj kon'tento /kon'tenta/]
I'm in love.	**Estoy enamorado /enamorada/.** [es'toj enamo'raðo /enamo'raða/]
I'm calm.	**Estoy tranquilo /tranquila/.** [es'toj traŋ'kilo /traŋ'kila/]
I'm bored.	**Estoy aburrido /aburrida/.** [es'toj aβu'riðo /aβu'riða/]
I'm tired.	**Estoy cansado /cansada/.** [es'toj kan'saðo /kan'saða/]
I'm sad.	**Estoy triste.** [es'toj 'triste]
I'm frightened.	**Estoy asustado /asustada/.** [es'toj asus'taðo /asus'taða/]
I'm angry.	**Estoy enfadado /enfadada/.** [es'toj eɱfa'ðaðo /eɱfa'ðaða/]
I'm worried.	**Estoy preocupado /preocupada/.** [es'toj preoku'paðo /preoku'paða/]
I'm nervous.	**Estoy nervioso /nerviosa/.** [es'toj ner'βjoθo /ner'βjoθa/]

I'm jealous. (envious)	**Estoy celoso /celosa/.** [es'toj θe'loθo /θe'loθa/]
I'm surprised.	**Estoy sorprendido /sorprendida/.** [es'toj sorpren'diðo /sorpren'diða/]
I'm perplexed.	**Estoy perplejo /perpleja/.** [es'toj per'pleχo /per'pleχa/]

Problems. Accidents

I've got a problem.
Tengo un problema.
[tengo un pro'βlema]

We've got a problem.
Tenemos un problema.
[te'nemos un pro'βlema]

I'm lost.
Estoy perdido /perdida/.
[es'toj per'ðiðo /per'ðiða/]

I missed the last bus (train).
Perdi el último autobús (tren).
[perði elʲ 'ulʲtimo auto'βus (tren)]

I don't have any money left.
No me queda más dinero.
[no me 'keða mas di'nero]

I've lost my ...
He perdido ...
[e per'ðiðo ...]

Someone stole my ...
Me han robado ...
[me an ro'βaðo ...]

passport
mi pasaporte
[mi pasa'porte]

wallet
mi cartera
[mi kar'tera]

papers
mis papeles
[mis pa'peles]

ticket
mi billete
[mi bi'jete]

---

money
mi dinero
[mi di'nero]

handbag
mi bolso
[mi 'bolʲso]

camera
mi cámara
[mi 'kamara]

laptop
mi portátil
[mi por'tatilʲ]

tablet computer
mi tableta
[mi ta'βleta]

mobile phone
mi teléfono
[mi te'lefono]

Help me!
¡Ayúdeme!
[a'juðeme!]

What's happened?
¿Qué pasó?
[ke pa'so?]

fire
el incendio
[elʲ in'θendjo]

English	Spanish	Pronunciation
shooting	**un tiroteo**	[un tiro'teo]
murder	**el asesinato**	[elʲ asesi'nato]
explosion	**una explosión**	[una eksIo'sjon]
fight	**una pelea**	[una pe'lea]
Call the police!	**¡Llame a la policía!**	[jame a lʲa poli'sia!]
Please hurry up!	**¡Más rápido, por favor!**	[mas 'rapiðo, por fa'βor!]
I'm looking for the police station.	**Busco la comisaría.**	[busko lʲa komisa'ria]
I need to make a call.	**Tengo que hacer una llamada.**	[tengo ke a'θer 'una ja'maða]
May I use your phone?	**¿Puedo usar su teléfono?**	[pu'eðo u'sar su te'lefono?]
I've been ...	**Me han ...**	[me an ...]
mugged	**asaltado /asaltada/**	[asalʲ'taðo /asalʲ'taða/]
robbed	**robado /robada/**	[ro'βaðo /ro'βaða/]
raped	**violada**	[bio'laða]
attacked (beaten up)	**atacado /atacada/**	[ata'kaðo /ata'kaða/]
Are you all right?	**¿Se encuentra bien?**	[se eŋku'entra bjen?]
Did you see who it was?	**¿Ha visto quien a sido?**	[a 'bisto kjen a 'siðo?]
Would you be able to recognize the person?	**¿Sería capaz de reconocer a la persona?**	[se'ria ka'paθ de rekono'θer a lʲa per'sona?]
Are you sure?	**¿Está usted seguro?**	[es'ta us'te se'ɣuro?]
Please calm down.	**Por favor, cálmese.**	[por fa'βor, 'kalʲmese]
Take it easy!	**¡Cálmese!**	[kalʲmese!]
Don't worry!	**¡No se preocupe!**	[no se preo'kupe!]
Everything will be fine.	**Todo irá bien.**	[toðo i'ra bjen]
Everything's all right.	**Todo está bien.**	[toðo es'ta bjen]

Come here, please.	**Venga aquí, por favor.** [benga a'ki, por fa'βor]
I have some questions for you.	**Tengo unas preguntas para usted.** [tengo 'unas pre'ɣuntas 'para us'te]
Wait a moment, please.	**Espere un momento, por favor.** [es'pere un mo'mento, por fa'βor]
Do you have any I.D.?	**¿Tiene un documento de identidad?** [tjene un doku'mento de iðenti'ðað?]
Thanks. You can leave now.	**Gracias. Puede irse ahora.** [graθjas. pu'eðe 'irse a'ora]
Hands behind your head!	**¡Manos detrás de la cabeza!** [manos de'tras de lʲa ka'βeθa!]
You're under arrest!	**¡Está arrestado /arrestada/!** [es'ta ares'taðo /ares'taða/!]

Health problems

Please help me.	**Ayudeme, por favor.** [a'juðeme, por fa'βor]
I don't feel well.	**No me encuentro bien.** [no me eŋku'entro bjen]
My husband doesn't feel well.	**Mi marido no se encuentra bien.** [mi ma'riðo no se eŋku'entra bjen]
My son ...	**Mi hijo ...** [mi 'iχo ...]
My father ...	**Mi padre ...** [mi 'paðre ...]
My wife doesn't feel well.	**Mi mujer no se encuentra bien.** [mi mu'χer no se eŋku'entra bjen]
My daughter ...	**Mi hija ...** [mi 'iχa ...]
My mother ...	**Mi madre ...** [mi 'maðre ...]
I've got a ...	**Me duele ...** [me du'ele ...]
headache	**la cabeza** [lʲa ka'βeθa]
sore throat	**la garganta** [lʲa gar'ɣanta]
stomach ache	**el estómago** [elʲ es'tomaɣo]
toothache	**un diente** [un 'djente]
I feel dizzy.	**Estoy mareado.** [es'toj mare'aðo]
He has a fever.	**Él tiene fiebre.** [elʲ 'tjene 'fjeβre]
She has a fever.	**Ella tiene fiebre.** [eja 'tjene 'fjeβre]
I can't breathe.	**No puedo respirar.** [no pu'eðo respi'rar]
I'm short of breath.	**Me ahogo.** [me a'oɣo]
I am asthmatic.	**Tengo asma.** [tengo 'asma]
I am diabetic.	**Tengo diabetes.** [tengo dja'βetes]

I can't sleep.	**No puedo dormir.** [no pu'eðo dor'mir]
food poisoning	**intoxicación alimentaria** [intoksika'θjon alimen'tarja]
It hurts here.	**Me duele aquí.** [me du'ele a'ki]
Help me!	**¡Ayúdeme!** [a'juðeme!]
I am here!	**¡Estoy aquí!** [es'toj a'ki!]
We are here!	**¡Estamos aquí!** [es'tamos a'ki!]
Get me out of here!	**¡Saquenme de aquí!** [sa'kenme de a'ki!]
I need a doctor.	**Necesito un médico.** [neθe'sito un 'meðiko]
I can't move.	**No me puedo mover.** [no me pu'eðo mo'βer]
I can't move my legs.	**No puedo mover mis piernas.** [no pu'eðo mo'βer mis 'pjernas]
I have a wound.	**Tengo una herida.** [tengo 'una e'riða]
Is it serious?	**¿Es grave?** [es 'graβe?]
My documents are in my pocket.	**Mis documentos están en mi bolsillo.** [mis doku'mentos es'tan en mi bol'sijo]
Calm down!	**¡Cálmese!** [kalʲmese!]
May I use your phone?	**¿Puedo usar su teléfono?** [pu'eðo u'sar su te'lefono?]
Call an ambulance!	**¡Llame a la ambulancia!** [jame a la ambu'lanθja!]
It's urgent!	**¡Es urgente!** [es ur'χente!]
It's an emergency!	**¡Es una emergencia!** [es 'una emer'χenθja!]
Please hurry up!	**¡Más rápido, por favor!** [mas 'rapiðo, por fa'βor!]
Would you please call a doctor?	**¿Puede llamar a un médico, por favor?** [pu'eðe ja'mar a un 'meðiko, por fa'βor?]
Where is the hospital?	**¿Dónde está el hospital?** [donde es'ta elʲ ospi'talʲ?]
How are you feeling?	**¿Cómo se siente?** [komo se 'sjente?]
Are you all right?	**¿Se encuentra bien?** [se eŋku'entra bjen?]

What's happened?	**¿Qué pasó?** [ke pa'so?]
I feel better now.	**Me encuentro mejor.** [me eŋku'entro me'χor]
It's OK.	**Está bien.** [es'ta bjen]
It's all right.	**Todo está bien.** [toðo es'ta bjen]

At the pharmacy

pharmacy (drugstore)	**la farmacia** [lʲa far'maθja]
24-hour pharmacy	**la farmacia 24 (veinte cuatro) horas** [lʲa far'maθja 'bejnte ku'atro 'oras]
Where is the closest pharmacy?	**¿Dónde está la farmacia más cercana?** [donde es'ta lʲa far'maθja mas θer'kana?]
Is it open now?	**¿Está abierta ahora?** [es'ta a'βjerta a'ora?]
At what time does it open?	**¿A qué hora abre?** [a ke 'ora 'aβre?]
At what time does it close?	**¿A qué hora cierra?** [a ke 'ora 'θjera?]
Is it far?	**¿Está lejos?** [es'ta 'leχos?]
Can I get there on foot?	**¿Puedo llegar a pie?** [pu'eðo je'ɣar a pje?]
Can you show me on the map?	**¿Puede mostrarme en el mapa?** [pu'eðe mos'trarme en elʲ 'mapa?]
Please give me something for ...	**Por favor, deme algo para ...** [por fa'βor, 'deme 'alʲɣo 'para ...]
a headache	**un dolor de cabeza** [un do'lor de ka'βeθa]
a cough	**la tos** [lʲa tos]
a cold	**el resfriado** [elʲ resfri'aðo]
the flu	**la gripe** [lʲa 'gripe]
a fever	**la fiebre** [lʲa 'fjeβre]
a stomach ache	**un dolor de estomago** [un do'lor de es'tomaɣo]
nausea	**nauseas** [nau'seas]
diarrhea	**la diarrea** [lʲa dja'rea]
constipation	**el estreñimiento** [elʲ estrenji'mjento]

pain in the back — **un dolor de espalda**
[un do'lor de es'palʲda]

chest pain — **un dolor de pecho**
[un do'lor de 'petʃo]

side stitch — **el flato**
[elʲ 'flato]

abdominal pain — **un dolor abdominal**
[un do'lor aβðomi'nalʲ]

---

pill — **la píldora**
[lʲa 'pilʲðora]

ointment, cream — **la crema**
[lʲa 'krema]

syrup — **el jarabe**
[elʲ χa'raβe]

spray — **el spray**
[elʲ spraj]

drops — **las gotas**
[lʲas 'gotas]

You need to go to the hospital. — **Tiene que ir al hospital.**
[tjene ke ir alʲ ospi'talʲ]

health insurance — **el seguro de salud**
[se'ɣuro de sa'lʲuð]

prescription — **la receta**
[re'θeta]

insect repellant — **el repelente de insectos**
[el repe'lente de in'sektos]

Band Aid — **la curita**
[lʲa ku'rita]

The bare minimum

Excuse me, ...	**Perdone, ...** [per'ðone, ...]
Hello.	**Hola.** [ola]
Thank you.	**Gracias.** [graθjas]
Good bye.	**Adiós.** [a'ðjos]
Yes.	**Sí.** [si]
No.	**No.** [no]
I don't know.	**No lo sé.** [no lo 'se]
Where? | Where to? | When?	**¿Dónde? | ¿A dónde? | ¿Cuándo?** [donde? | a 'donde? | ku'ando?]

I need ...	**Necesito ...** [neθe'sito ...]
I want ...	**Quiero ...** [kjero ...]
Do you have ...?	**¿Tiene ...?** [tjene ...?]
Is there a ... here?	**¿Hay ... por aquí?** [aj ... por a'ki?]
May I ...?	**¿Puedo ...?** [pu'eðo ...?]
..., please (polite request)	**..., por favor** [..., por fa'βor]

I'm looking for ...	**Busco ...** [busko ...]
the restroom	**el servicio** [elʲ ser'βiθjo]
an ATM	**un cajero** [un ka'χero]
a pharmacy (drugstore)	**una farmacia** [una far'maθja]
a hospital	**el hospital** [elʲ ospi'talʲ]
the police station	**la comisaría** [lʲa komisa'ria]
the subway	**el metro** [elʲ 'metro]

a taxi	**un taxi** [un 'taksi]
the train station	**la estación de tren** [lʲa esta'θjon de tren]

My name is ...	**Me llamo ...** [me 'jamo ...]
What's your name?	**¿Cómo se llama?** [komo se 'jama?]
Could you please help me?	**¿Puede ayudarme, por favor?** [pu'eðe aju'ðarme, por fa'βor?]
I've got a problem.	**Tengo un problema.** [tengo un pro'βlema]
I don't feel well.	**Me encuentro mal.** [me eŋku'entro malʲ]
Call an ambulance!	**¡Llame a la ambulancia!** [jame a la ambu'lanθja!]
May I make a call?	**¿Puedo llamar, por favor?** [pu'eðo ja'mar, por fa'βor?]

I'm sorry.	**Lo siento.** [lo 'sjento]
You're welcome.	**De nada.** [ðe 'naða]

I, me	**Yo** [jo]
you (inform.)	**tú** [tu]
he	**él** [elʲ]
she	**ella** [eja]
they (masc.)	**ellos** [ejos]
they (fem.)	**ellas** [ejas]
we	**nosotros** [no'sotros]
you (pl)	**ustedes | vosotros** [us'teðes | bo'sotros]
you (sg, form.)	**usted** [us'teð]

ENTRANCE	**ENTRADA** [en'traða]
EXIT	**SALIDA** [sa'liða]
OUT OF ORDER	**FUERA DE SERVICIO** [fu'era de ser'βiθjo]
CLOSED	**CERRADO** [θe'raðo]

OPEN	**ABIERTO** [a'βjerto]
FOR WOMEN	**PARA SEÑORAS** [para se'njoras]
FOR MEN	**PARA CABALLEROS** [para kaβa'jeros]

TOPICAL VOCABULARY

This section contains more than 3,000 of the most important words.
The dictionary will provide invaluable assistance while traveling abroad, because frequently individual words are enough for you to be understood.
The dictionary includes a convenient transcription of each foreign word

T&P Books Publishing

VOCABULARY CONTENTS

T&P Books Publishing

BASIC CONCEPTS

T&P Books Publishing

1. Pronouns

I, me	**yo**	[jo]
you	**tú**	[tu]
he	**él**	[elʲ]
she	**ella**	['eja]
we (masc.)	**nosotros**	[no'sotros]
we (fem.)	**nosotras**	[no'sotras]
you (masc.)	**vosotros**	[bo'sotros]
you (fem.)	**vosotras**	[bo'sotras]
you (polite, sing.)	**Usted**	[us'teð]
you (polite, pl)	**Ustedes**	[us'teðes]
they (masc.)	**ellos**	['ejos]
they (fem.)	**ellas**	['ejas]

2. Greetings. Salutations

Hello! (fam.)	**¡Hola!**	['olʲa]
Hello! (form.)	**¡Hola!**	['olʲa]
Good morning!	**¡Buenos días!**	['buenos 'dias]
Good afternoon!	**¡Buenas tardes!**	['buenas 'tarðes]
Good evening!	**¡Buenas noches!**	['buenas 'notʃes]
to say hello	**decir hola**	[de'θir 'olʲa]
Hi! (hello)	**¡Hola!**	['olʲa]
greeting (n)	**saludo** (m)	[sa'lʲuðo]
to greet (vt)	**saludar** (vt)	[salʲu'ðar]
How are you?	**¿Cómo estás?**	['komo es'tas]
What's new?	**¿Qué hay de nuevo?**	[ke aj de nu'eβo]
Goodbye!	**¡Adiós!**	[a'ðjos]
Bye!	**¡Hasta la vista!**	['asta lʲa 'bista]
See you soon!	**¡Hasta pronto!**	['asta 'pronto]
Farewell!	**¡Adiós!**	[a'ðjos]
to say goodbye	**despedirse** (vr)	[despe'ðirse]
So long!	**¡Hasta luego!**	['asta lʲu'eɣo]
Thank you!	**¡Gracias!**	['graθjas]
Thank you very much!	**¡Muchas gracias!**	['mutʃas 'graθjas]
You're welcome	**De nada**	[de 'naða]
Don't mention it!	**No hay de qué**	[no aj de 'ke]
It was nothing	**De nada**	[de 'naða]

Excuse me! (fam.)	**¡Disculpa!**	[dis'kulʲpa]
Excuse me! (form.)	**¡Disculpe!**	[dis'kulʲpe]
to excuse (forgive)	**disculpar** (vt)	[diskulʲ'par]

to apologize (vi)	**disculparse** (vr)	[diskulʲ'parse]
My apologies	**Mis disculpas**	[mis dis'kulʲpas]
I'm sorry!	**¡Perdóneme!**	[per'ðoneme]
to forgive (vt)	**perdonar** (vt)	[perðo'nar]
It's okay! (that's all right)	**¡No pasa nada!**	[no 'pasa 'naða]
please (adv)	**por favor**	[por fa'βor]

Don't forget!	**¡No se le olvide!**	[no se le olʲ'βiðe]
Certainly!	**¡Ciertamente!**	[θjerta'mento]
Of course not!	**¡Claro que no!**	['klʲaro ke 'no]
Okay! (I agree)	**¡De acuerdo!**	[de aku'erðo]
That's enough!	**¡Basta!**	['basta]

3. Questions

Who?	**¿Quién?**	['kjen]
What?	**¿Qué?**	[ke]
Where? (at, in)	**¿Dónde?**	['donde]
Where (to)?	**¿Adónde?**	[a'ðonde]
From where?	**¿De dónde?**	[de 'donde]
When?	**¿Cuándo?**	[ku'ando]
Why? (What for?)	**¿Para qué?**	[para 'ke]
Why? (~ are you crying?)	**¿Por qué?**	[por 'ke]

What for?	**¿Por qué razón?**	[por ke ra'θon]
How? (in what way)	**¿Cómo?**	['komo]
Which?	**¿Cuál?**	[ku'alʲ]

To whom?	**¿A quién?**	[a 'kjen]
About whom?	**¿De quién?**	[de 'kjen]
About what?	**¿De qué?**	[de 'ke]
With whom?	**¿Con quién?**	[kon 'kjen]

How many? How much?	**¿Cuánto?**	[ku'anto]
Whose?	**¿De quién?**	[de 'kjen]

4. Prepositions

with (accompanied by)	**con ...**	[kon]
without	**sin**	[sin]
to (indicating direction)	**a ...**	[a]
about (talking ~ ...)	**de ..., sobre ...**	[de], ['soβre]
before (in time)	**antes de ...**	['antes de]
in front of ...	**delante de ...**	[de'lʲante de]

under (beneath, below)	**debajo de ...**	[de'βaχo de]
above (over)	**sobre ..., encima de ...**	['soβre], [en'θima de]
on (atop)	**en ..., sobre ...**	[en], ['soβre]
from (off, out of)	**de ...**	[de]
of (made from)	**de ...**	[de]
in (e.g., ~ ten minutes)	**dentro de ...**	['dentro de]
over (across the top of)	**encima de ...**	[en'θima de]

5. Function words. Adverbs. Part 1

Where? (at, in)	**¿Dónde?**	['donde]
here (adv)	**aquí** (adv)	[a'ki]
there (adv)	**allí** (adv)	[a'ji]
somewhere (to be)	**en alguna parte**	[en alʲ'ɣuna 'parte]
nowhere (not anywhere)	**en ninguna parte**	[en nin'guna 'parte]
by (near, beside)	**junto a ...**	['χunto a]
by the window	**junto a la ventana**	['χunto a lʲa ben'tana]
Where (to)?	**¿Adónde?**	[a'ðonde]
here (e.g., come ~!)	**aquí** (adv)	[a'ki]
there (e.g., to go ~)	**allí** (adv)	[a'ji]
from here (adv)	**de aquí** (adv)	[de a'ki]
from there (adv)	**de allí** (adv)	[de a'ji]
close (adv)	**cerca**	['θerka]
far (adv)	**lejos** (adv)	['leχos]
near (e.g., ~ Paris)	**cerca de ...**	['θerka de]
nearby (adv)	**al lado de ...**	[alʲ 'lʲaðo de]
not far (adv)	**no lejos** (adv)	[no 'leχos]
left (adj)	**izquierdo** (adj)	[iθ'kjerðo]
on the left	**a la izquierda**	[a lʲa iθ'kjerða]
to the left	**a la izquierda**	[a lʲa iθ'kjerða]
right (adj)	**derecho** (adj)	[de'reʧo]
on the right	**a la derecha**	[a lʲa de'reʧa]
to the right	**a la derecha**	[a lʲa de'reʧa]
in front (adv)	**delante**	[de'lʲante]
front (as adj)	**delantero** (adj)	[delʲan'tero]
ahead (the kids ran ~)	**adelante**	[aðe'lʲante]
behind (adv)	**detrás de ...**	[de'tras de]
from behind	**desde atrás**	['desðe a'tras]
back (towards the rear)	**atrás**	[a'tras]
middle	**centro** (m), **medio** (m)	['θentro], ['meðjo]

in the middle	**en medio** (adv)	[en 'meðjo]
at the side	**de lado** (adv)	[de 'laðo]
everywhere (adv)	**en todas partes**	[en 'toðas 'partes]
around (in all directions)	**alrededor** (adv)	[alʲreðe'ðor]
from inside	**de dentro** (adv)	[de 'dentro]
somewhere (to go)	**a alguna parte**	[a alʲ'ɣuna 'parte]
straight (directly)	**todo derecho** (adv)	['toðo de'reʧo]
back (e.g., come ~)	**atrás**	[a'tras]
from anywhere	**de alguna parte**	[de alʲ'ɣuna 'parte]
from somewhere	**de alguna parte**	[de alʲ'ɣuna 'parte]
firstly (adv)	**primero** (adv)	[pri'mero]
secondly (adv)	**segundo** (adv)	[se'ɣundo]
thirdly (adv)	**tercero** (adv)	[ter'θero]
suddenly (adv)	**de súbito** (adv)	[de 'suβito]
at first (in the beginning)	**al principio** (adv)	[alʲ prin'θipjo]
for the first time	**por primera vez**	[por pri'mera beθ]
long before ...	**mucho tiempo antes ...**	['muʧo 'tjempo 'antes]
anew (over again)	**de nuevo** (adv)	[de nu'eβo]
for good (adv)	**para siempre** (adv)	['para 'sjempre]
never (adv)	**nunca** (adv)	['nuŋka]
again (adv)	**de nuevo** (adv)	[de nu'eβo]
now (adv)	**ahora** (adv)	[a'ora]
often (adv)	**frecuentemente** (adv)	[frekuente'mente]
then (adv)	**entonces** (adv)	[en'tonθes]
urgently (quickly)	**urgentemente**	[urχente'mente]
usually (adv)	**usualmente** (adv)	[usualʲ'mente]
by the way, ...	**a propósito, ...**	[a pro'posito]
possible (that is ~)	**es probable**	[es pro'βaβle]
probably (adv)	**probablemente**	[proβaβle'mente]
maybe (adv)	**tal vez**	[talʲ beθ]
besides ...	**además ...**	[aðe'mas]
that's why ...	**por eso ...**	[por 'eso]
in spite of ...	**a pesar de ...**	[a pe'sar de]
thanks to ...	**gracias a ...**	['graθjas a]
what (pron.)	**qué**	[ke]
that (conj.)	**que**	[ke]
something	**algo**	['alʲɣo]
anything (something)	**algo**	['alʲɣo]
nothing	**nada**	['naða]
who (pron.)	**quien**	[kjen]
someone	**alguien**	['alʲɣjen]
somebody	**alguien**	['alʲɣjen]
nobody	**nadie**	['naðje]
nowhere (a voyage to ~)	**a ninguna parte**	[a nin'guna 'parte]

nobody's	**de nadie**	[de 'naðje]
somebody's	**de alguien**	[de 'alʲɣjen]
so (I'm ~ glad)	**tan, tanto** (adv)	[tan], ['tanto]
also (as well)	**también**	[tam'bjen]
too (as well)	**también**	[tam'bjen]

6. Function words. Adverbs. Part 2

Why?	**¿Por qué?**	[por 'ke]
for some reason	**por alguna razón**	[por alʲ'ɣuna ra'θon]
because ...	**porque ...**	['porke]
for some purpose	**por cualquier razón** (adv)	[por kualʲ'kjer ra'θon]
and	**y**	[i]
or	**o**	[o]
but	**pero**	['pero]
for (e.g., ~ me)	**para**	['para]
too (~ many people)	**demasiado** (adv)	[dema'sjaðo]
only (exclusively)	**sólo, solamente** (adv)	['solo], [solʲa'mente]
exactly (adv)	**exactamente** (adv)	[eksakta'mente]
about (more or less)	**cerca de ...**	['θerka de]
approximately (adv)	**aproximadamente**	[aproksimaða'mente]
approximate (adj)	**aproximado** (adj)	[aproksi'maðo]
almost (adv)	**casi** (adv)	['kasi]
the rest	**resto** (m)	['resto]
each (adj)	**cada** (adj)	['kaða]
any (no matter which)	**cualquier** (adj)	[kualʲ'kjer]
many, much (a lot of)	**mucho** (adv)	['mutʃo]
many people	**mucha gente**	['mutʃa 'χente]
all (everyone)	**todos**	['toðos]
in return for ...	**a cambio de ...**	[a 'kambjo de]
in exchange (adv)	**en cambio** (adv)	[en 'kambjo]
by hand (made)	**a mano**	[a 'mano]
hardly (negative opinion)	**poco probable**	['poko pro'βaβle]
probably (adv)	**probablemente**	[proβaβle'mente]
on purpose (intentionally)	**a propósito** (adv)	[a pro'posito]
by accident (adv)	**por accidente** (adv)	[por akθi'ðente]
very (adv)	**muy** (adv)	['muj]
for example (adv)	**por ejemplo** (adv)	[por e'χemplo]
between	**entre**	['entre]
among	**entre**	['entre]
so much (such a lot)	**tanto**	['tanto]
especially (adv)	**especialmente** (adv)	[espeθjalʲ'mente]

NUMBERS. MISCELLANEOUS

T&P Books Publishing

7. Cardinal numbers. Part 1

0 zero	**cero**	['θero]
1 one	**uno**	['uno]
2 two	**dos**	[dos]
3 three	**tres**	[tres]
4 four	**cuatro**	[ku'atro]
5 five	**cinco**	['θiŋko]
6 six	**seis**	['sejs]
7 seven	**siete**	['sjete]
8 eight	**ocho**	['otʃo]
9 nine	**nueve**	[nu'eβe]
10 ten	**diez**	[djeθ]
11 eleven	**once**	['onθe]
12 twelve	**doce**	['doθe]
13 thirteen	**trece**	['treθe]
14 fourteen	**catorce**	[ka'torθe]
15 fifteen	**quince**	['kinθe]
16 sixteen	**dieciséis**	['djeθi·s'ejs]
17 seventeen	**diecisiete**	['djeθi·'sjete]
18 eighteen	**dieciocho**	['djeθi·'otʃo]
19 nineteen	**diecinueve**	['djeθi·nu'eβe]
20 twenty	**veinte**	['bejnte]
21 twenty-one	**veintiuno**	[bejnti·'uno]
22 twenty-two	**veintidós**	[bejnti·'dos]
23 twenty-three	**veintitrés**	[bejnti·'tres]
30 thirty	**treinta**	['trejnta]
31 thirty-one	**treinta y uno**	['trejnta i 'uno]
32 thirty-two	**treinta y dos**	['trejnta i 'dos]
33 thirty-three	**treinta y tres**	['trejnta i 'tres]
40 forty	**cuarenta**	[kua'renta]
41 forty-one	**cuarenta y uno**	[kua'renta i 'uno]
42 forty-two	**cuarenta y dos**	[kua'renta i 'dos]
43 forty-three	**cuarenta y tres**	[kua'renta i 'tres]
50 fifty	**cincuenta**	[θiŋku'enta]
51 fifty-one	**cincuenta y uno**	[θiŋku'enta i 'uno]
52 fifty-two	**cincuenta y dos**	[θiŋku'enta i 'dos]
53 fifty-three	**cincuenta y tres**	[θiŋku'enta i 'tres]
60 sixty	**sesenta**	[se'senta]

61 sixty-one	**sesenta y uno**	[se'senta i 'uno]
62 sixty-two	**sesenta y dos**	[se'senta i 'dos]
63 sixty-three	**sesenta y tres**	[se'senta i 'tres]
70 seventy	**setenta**	[se'tenta]
71 seventy-one	**setenta y uno**	[se'tenta i 'uno]
72 seventy-two	**setenta y dos**	[se'tenta i 'dos]
73 seventy-three	**setenta y tres**	[se'tenta i 'tres]
80 eighty	**ochenta**	[o'ʧenta]
81 eighty-one	**ochenta y uno**	[o'ʧenta i 'uno]
82 eighty-two	**ochenta y dos**	[o'ʧenta i 'dos]
83 eighty-three	**ochenta y tres**	[o'ʧenta i 'tres]
90 ninety	**noventa**	[no'βenta]
91 ninety-one	**noventa y uno**	[no'βenta i 'uno]
92 ninety-two	**noventa y dos**	[no'βenta i 'dos]
93 ninety-three	**noventa y tres**	[no'βenta i 'tres]

8. Cardinal numbers. Part 2

100 one hundred	**cien**	[θjen]
200 two hundred	**doscientos**	[doθ·'θjentos]
300 three hundred	**trescientos**	[treθ·'θjentos]
400 four hundred	**cuatrocientos**	[ku'atro·'θjentos]
500 five hundred	**quinientos**	[ki'njentos]
600 six hundred	**seiscientos**	[sejs·'θjentos]
700 seven hundred	**setecientos**	[θete·'θjentos]
800 eight hundred	**ochocientos**	[oʧo·'θjentos]
900 nine hundred	**novecientos**	[noβe·'θjentos]
1000 one thousand	**mil**	[milʲ]
2000 two thousand	**dos mil**	['dos 'milʲ]
3000 three thousand	**tres mil**	['tres 'milʲ]
10000 ten thousand	**diez mil**	['djeθ 'milʲ]
one hundred thousand	**cien mil**	['θjen 'milʲ]
million	**millón** (m)	[mi'jon]
billion	**mil millones**	[milʲ mi'jones]

9. Ordinal numbers

first (adj)	**primero** (adj)	[pri'mero]
second (adj)	**segundo** (adj)	[se'ɣundo]
third (adj)	**tercero** (adj)	[ter'θero]
fourth (adj)	**cuarto** (adj)	[ku'arto]
fifth (adj)	**quinto** (adj)	['kinto]
sixth (adj)	**sexto** (adj)	['seksto]

seventh (adj)	**séptimo** (adj)	['septimo]
eighth (adj)	**octavo** (adj)	[ok'taβo]
ninth (adj)	**noveno** (adj)	[no'βeno]
tenth (adj)	**décimo** (adj)	['deθimo]

COLOURS. UNITS OF MEASUREMENT

T&P Books Publishing

10. Colors

color	**color** (m)	[ko'lor]
shade (tint)	**matiz** (m)	[ma'tiθ]
hue	**tono** (m)	['tono]
rainbow	**arco** (m) **iris**	['arko 'iris]
white (adj)	**blanco** (adj)	['blʲaŋko]
black (adj)	**negro** (adj)	['neɣro]
gray (adj)	**gris** (adj)	['gris]
green (adj)	**verde** (adj)	['berðe]
yellow (adj)	**amarillo** (adj)	[ama'rijo]
red (adj)	**rojo** (adj)	['roχo]
blue (adj)	**azul** (adj)	[a'θulʲ]
light blue (adj)	**azul claro** (adj)	[a'θulʲ 'klʲaro]
pink (adj)	**rosa** (adj)	['rosa]
orange (adj)	**naranja** (adj)	[na'ranχa]
violet (adj)	**violeta** (adj)	[bio'leta]
brown (adj)	**marrón** (adj)	[ma'ron]
golden (adj)	**dorado** (adj)	[do'raðo]
silvery (adj)	**argentado** (adj)	[arχen'taðo]
beige (adj)	**beige** (adj)	['bejs]
cream (adj)	**crema** (adj)	['krema]
turquoise (adj)	**turquesa** (adj)	[tur'kesa]
cherry red (adj)	**rojo cereza** (adj)	['roχo θe'reθa]
lilac (adj)	**lila** (adj)	['lilʲa]
crimson (adj)	**carmesí** (adj)	[karme'si]
light (adj)	**claro** (adj)	['klʲaro]
dark (adj)	**oscuro** (adj)	[os'kuro]
bright, vivid (adj)	**vivo** (adj)	['biβo]
colored (pencils)	**de color** (adj)	[de ko'lor]
color (e.g., ~ film)	**en colores** (adj)	[en ko'lores]
black-and-white (adj)	**blanco y negro** (adj)	['blʲaŋko i 'neɣro]
plain (one-colored)	**unicolor** (adj)	[uniko'lor]
multicolored (adj)	**multicolor** (adj)	[mulʲtiko'lor]

11. Units of measurement

weight	**peso** (m)	['peso]
length	**longitud** (f)	[lonχi'tuð]

width	**anchura** (f)	[an'tʃura]
height	**altura** (f)	[alʲ'tura]
depth	**profundidad** (f)	[profundi'ðað]
volume	**volumen** (m)	[bo'lʲumen]
area	**área** (f)	['area]
gram	**gramo** (m)	['gramo]
milligram	**miligramo** (m)	[mili'ɣramo]
kilogram	**kilogramo** (m)	[kilo'ɣramo]
ton	**tonelada** (f)	[tone'lʲaða]
pound	**libra** (f)	['liβra]
ounce	**onza** (f)	['onθa]
meter	**metro** (m)	['metro]
millimeter	**milímetro** (m)	[mi'limetro]
centimeter	**centímetro** (m)	[θen'timetro]
kilometer	**kilómetro** (m)	[ki'lometro]
mile	**milla** (f)	['mija]
inch	**pulgada** (f)	[pulʲ'ɣaða]
foot	**pie** (m)	[pje]
yard	**yarda** (f)	['jarða]
square meter	**metro** (m) **cuadrado**	['metro kua'ðraðo]
hectare	**hectárea** (f)	[ek'tarea]
liter	**litro** (m)	['litro]
degree	**grado** (m)	['graðo]
volt	**voltio** (m)	['bolʲtjo]
ampere	**amperio** (m)	[am'perjo]
horsepower	**caballo** (m) **de fuerza**	[ka'βajo de fu'erθa]
quantity	**cantidad** (f)	[kanti'ðað]
a little bit of ...	**un poco de ...**	[un 'poko de]
half	**mitad** (f)	[mi'tað]
dozen	**docena** (f)	[do'θena]
piece (item)	**pieza** (f)	['pjeθa]
size	**dimensión** (f)	[dimen'sjon]
scale (map ~)	**escala** (f)	[es'kalʲa]
minimal (adj)	**mínimo** (adj)	['minimo]
the smallest (adj)	**el más pequeño** (adj)	[elʲ mas pe'kenjo]
medium (adj)	**medio** (adj)	['meðjo]
maximal (adj)	**máximo** (adj)	['maksimo]
the largest (adj)	**el más grande** (adj)	[elʲ 'mas 'grande]

12. Containers

canning jar (glass ~)	**tarro** (m) **de vidrio**	['taro de 'biðrjo]
can	**lata** (f)	['lʲata]

bucket	**cubo** (m)	['kuβo]
barrel	**barril** (m)	[ba'rilʲ]
wash basin (e.g., plastic ~)	**palangana** (f)	[palʲan'gana]
tank (100L water ~)	**tanque** (m)	['taŋke]
hip flask	**petaca** (f)	[pe'taka]
jerrycan	**bidón** (m) **de gasolina**	[bi'ðon de gaso'lina]
tank (e.g., tank car)	**cisterna** (f)	[θis'terna]
mug	**taza** (f)	['taθa]
cup (of coffee, etc.)	**taza** (f)	['taθa]
saucer	**platillo** (m)	[plʲa'tijo]
glass (tumbler)	**vaso** (m)	['baso]
wine glass	**copa** (f) **de vino**	['kopa de 'bino]
stock pot (soup pot)	**olla** (f)	['oja]
bottle (~ of wine)	**botella** (f)	[bo'teja]
neck (of the bottle, etc.)	**cuello** (m) **de botella**	[ku'ejo de bo'teja]
carafe (decanter)	**garrafa** (f)	[ga'rafa]
pitcher	**jarro** (m)	['χaro]
vessel (container)	**recipiente** (m)	[reθi'pjente]
pot (crock, stoneware ~)	**tarro** (m)	['taro]
vase	**florero** (m)	[flo'rero]
bottle (perfume ~)	**frasco** (m)	['frasko]
vial, small bottle	**frasquito** (m)	[fras'kito]
tube (of toothpaste)	**tubo** (m)	['tuβo]
sack (bag)	**saco** (m)	['sako]
bag (paper ~, plastic ~)	**bolsa** (f)	['bolʲsa]
pack (of cigarettes, etc.)	**paquete** (m)	[pa'kete]
box (e.g., shoebox)	**caja** (f)	['kaχa]
crate	**caja** (f)	['kaχa]
basket	**cesta** (f)	['θesta]

MAIN VERBS

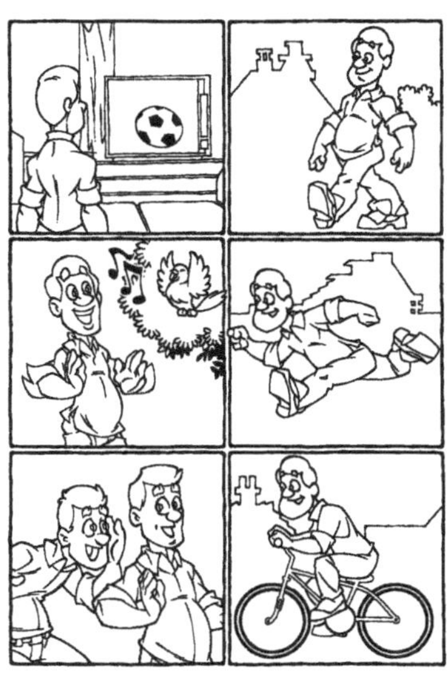

T&P Books Publishing

13. The most important verbs. Part 1

to advise (vt)	**aconsejar** (vt)	[akonse'χar]
to agree (say yes)	**estar de acuerdo**	[es'tar de aku'erðo]
to answer (vi, vt)	**responder** (vi, vt)	[respon'der]
to arrive (vi)	**llegar** (vi)	[je'ɣar]
to ask (~ oneself)	**preguntar** (vt)	[preɣun'tar]
to ask (~ sb to do sth)	**pedir** (vt)	[pe'ðir]
to be (~ a teacher)	**ser** (vi)	[ser]
to be (~ on a diet)	**estar** (vi)	[es'tar]
to be afraid	**tener miedo**	[te'ner 'mjeðo]
to be hungry	**tener hambre**	[te'ner 'ambre]
to be interested in ...	**interesarse** (vr)	[intere'sarse]
to be needed	**ser necesario**	[ser neθe'sarjo]
to be surprised	**sorprenderse** (vr)	[sorpren'derse]
to be thirsty	**tener sed**	[te'ner 'seð]
to begin (vt)	**comenzar** (vi, vt)	[komen'θar]
to belong to ...	**pertenecer a ...**	[pertene'θer a]
to boast (vi)	**jactarse, alabarse** (vr)	[χas'tarse], [alʲa'βarse]
to break (split into pieces)	**quebrar** (vt)	[ke'βrar]
to call (~ for help)	**llamar** (vt)	[ja'mar]
can (v aux)	**poder** (v aux)	[po'ðer]
to catch (vt)	**coger** (vt)	[ko'χer]
to change (vt)	**cambiar** (vt)	[kam'bjar]
to choose (select)	**escoger** (vt)	[esko'χer]
to come down (the stairs)	**descender** (vi)	[deθen'der]
to compare (vt)	**comparar** (vt)	[kompa'rar]
to complain (vi, vt)	**quejarse** (vr)	[ke'χarse]
to confuse (mix up)	**confundir** (vt)	[koɱfun'dir]
to continue (vt)	**continuar** (vt)	[kontinu'ar]
to control (vt)	**controlar** (vt)	[kontro'lʲar]
to cook (dinner)	**preparar** (vt)	[prepa'rar]
to cost (vt)	**costar** (vt)	[kos'tar]
to count (add up)	**contar** (vt)	[kon'tar]
to count on ...	**contar con ...**	[kon'tar kon]
to create (vt)	**crear** (vt)	[kre'ar]
to cry (weep)	**llorar** (vi)	[jo'rar]

14. The most important verbs. Part 2

to deceive (vi, vt)	**engañar** (vi, vt)	[enga'njar]
to decorate (tree, street)	**decorar** (vt)	[deko'rar]
to defend (a country, etc.)	**defender** (vt)	[ðefen'der]
to demand (request firmly)	**exigir** (vt)	[eksi'χir]
to dig (vt)	**cavar** (vt)	[ka'βar]
to discuss (vt)	**discutir** (vt)	[disku'tir]
to do (vt)	**hacer** (vt)	[a'θer]
to doubt (have doubts)	**dudar** (vt)	[du'ðar]
to drop (let fall)	**dejar caer**	[de'χar ka'er]
to enter (room, house, etc.)	**entrar** (vi)	[en'trar]
to excuse (forgive)	**disculpar** (vt)	[diskulʲ'par]
to exist (vi)	**existir** (vi)	[eksis'tir]
to expect (foresee)	**prever** (vt)	[pre'βer]
to explain (vt)	**explicar** (vt)	[ekspli'kar]
to fall (vi)	**caer** (vi)	[ka'er]
to find (vt)	**encontrar** (vt)	[eŋkon'trar]
to finish (vt)	**acabar, terminar** (vt)	[aka'βar], [termi'nar]
to fly (vi)	**volar** (vi)	[bo'lʲar]
to follow ... (come after)	**seguir ...**	[se'ɣir]
to forget (vi, vt)	**olvidar** (vt)	[olʲβi'ðar]
to forgive (vt)	**perdonar** (vt)	[perðo'nar]
to give (vt)	**dar** (vt)	[dar]
to give a hint	**dar una pista**	[dar 'una 'pista]
to go (on foot)	**ir** (vi)	[ir]
to go for a swim	**bañarse** (vr)	[ba'njarse]
to go out (for dinner, etc.)	**salir** (vi)	[sa'lir]
to guess (the answer)	**adivinar** (vt)	[aðiβi'nar]
to have (vt)	**tener** (vt)	[te'ner]
to have breakfast	**desayunar** (vi)	[desaju'nar]
to have dinner	**cenar** (vi)	[θe'nar]
to have lunch	**almorzar** (vi)	[alʲmor'θar]
to hear (vt)	**oír** (vt)	[o'ir]
to help (vt)	**ayudar** (vt)	[aju'ðar]
to hide (vt)	**esconder** (vt)	[eskon'der]
to hope (vi, vt)	**esperar** (vi)	[espe'rar]
to hunt (vi, vt)	**cazar** (vi, vt)	[ka'θar]
to hurry (vi)	**tener prisa**	[te'ner 'prisa]

15. The most important verbs. Part 3

to inform (vt)	**informar** (vt)	[iɱfor'mar]
to insist (vi, vt)	**insistir** (vi)	[insis'tir]
to insult (vt)	**insultar** (vt)	[insulʲ'tar]
to invite (vt)	**invitar** (vt)	[imbi'tar]
to joke (vi)	**bromear** (vi)	[brome'ar]
to keep (vt)	**guardar** (vt)	[guar'ðar]
to keep silent	**callarse** (vr)	[ka'jarse]
to kill (vt)	**matar** (vt)	[ma'tar]
to know (sb)	**conocer** (vt)	[kono'θer]
to know (sth)	**saber** (vt)	[sa'βer]
to laugh (vi)	**reírse** (vr)	[re'irse]
to liberate (city, etc.)	**liberar** (vt)	[liβe'rar]
to like (I like ...)	**gustar** (vi)	[gus'tar]
to look for ... (search)	**buscar** (vt)	[bus'kar]
to love (sb)	**querer, amar** (vt)	[ke'rer], [a'mar]
to make a mistake	**equivocarse** (vr)	[ekiβo'karse]
to manage, to run	**dirigir** (vt)	[diri'χir]
to mean (signify)	**significar** (vt)	[siɣnifi'kar]
to mention (talk about)	**mencionar** (vt)	[menθjo'nar]
to miss (school, etc.)	**faltar a ...**	[falʲ'tar a]
to notice (see)	**percibir** (vt)	[perθi'βir]
to object (vi, vt)	**objetar** (vt)	[oβχe'tar]
to observe (see)	**observar** (vt)	[oβser'βar]
to open (vt)	**abrir** (vt)	[a'βrir]
to order (meal, etc.)	**pedir** (vt)	[pe'ðir]
to order (mil.)	**ordenar** (vt)	[orðe'nar]
to own (possess)	**poseer** (vt)	[pose'er]
to participate (vi)	**participar** (vi)	[partiθi'par]
to pay (vi, vt)	**pagar** (vi, vt)	[pa'ɣar]
to permit (vt)	**permitir** (vt)	[permi'tir]
to plan (vt)	**planear** (vt)	[plʲane'ar]
to play (children)	**jugar** (vi)	[χu'ɣar]
to pray (vi, vt)	**orar** (vi)	[o'rar]
to prefer (vt)	**preferir** (vt)	[prefe'rir]
to promise (vt)	**prometer** (vt)	[prome'ter]
to pronounce (vt)	**pronunciar** (vt)	[pronun'θjar]
to propose (vt)	**proponer** (vt)	[propo'ner]
to punish (vt)	**punir, castigar** (vt)	[pu'nir], [kasti'ɣar]

16. The most important verbs. Part 4

to read (vi, vt)	**leer** (vi, vt)	[le'er]
to recommend (vt)	**recomendar** (vt)	[rekomen'dar]

to refuse (vi, vt)	**negarse** (vr)	[ne'ɣarse]
to regret (be sorry)	**arrepentirse** (vr)	[arepen'tirse]
to rent (sth from sb)	**alquilar** (vt)	[alʲki'lʲar]
to repeat (say again)	**repetir** (vt)	[repe'tir]
to reserve, to book	**reservar** (vt)	[reser'βar]
to run (vi)	**correr** (vi)	[ko'rer]
to save (rescue)	**salvar** (vt)	[salʲ'βar]
to say (~ thank you)	**decir** (vt)	[de'θir]
to scold (vt)	**regañar, reprender** (vt)	[reɣa'njar], [repren'der]
to see (vt)	**ver** (vt)	[ber]
to sell (vt)	**vender** (vt)	[ben'der]
to send (vt)	**enviar** (vt)	[em'bjar]
to shoot (vi)	**disparar, tirar** (vi)	[dispa'rar], [ti'rar]
to shout (vi)	**gritar** (vi)	[gri'tar]
to show (vt)	**mostrar** (vt)	[mos'trar]
to sign (document)	**firmar** (vt)	[fir'mar]
to sit down (vi)	**sentarse** (vr)	[sen'tarse]
to smile (vi)	**sonreír** (vi)	[sonre'ir]
to speak (vi, vt)	**hablar** (vi, vt)	[a'βlʲar]
to steal (money, etc.)	**robar** (vt)	[ro'βar]
to stop (for pause, etc.)	**pararse** (vr)	[pa'rarse]
to stop (please ~ calling me)	**cesar** (vt)	[θe'sar]
to study (vt)	**estudiar** (vt)	[estu'ðjar]
to swim (vi)	**nadar** (vi)	[na'ðar]
to take (vt)	**tomar** (vt)	[to'mar]
to think (vi, vt)	**pensar** (vi, vt)	[pen'sar]
to threaten (vt)	**amenazar** (vt)	[amena'θar]
to touch (with hands)	**tocar** (vt)	[to'kar]
to translate (vt)	**traducir** (vt)	[traðu'θir]
to trust (vt)	**confiar** (vt)	[koɱ'fjar]
to try (attempt)	**probar, tentar** (vt)	[pro'βar], [ten'tar]
to turn (e.g., ~ left)	**girar** (vi)	[χi'rar]
to underestimate (vt)	**subestimar** (vt)	[suβesti'mar]
to understand (vt)	**comprender** (vt)	[kompren'der]
to unite (vt)	**unir** (vt)	[u'nir]
to wait (vt)	**esperar** (vt)	[espe'rar]
to want (wish, desire)	**querer** (vt)	[ke'rer]
to warn (vt)	**advertir** (vt)	[aðβer'tir]
to work (vi)	**trabajar** (vi)	[traβa'χar]
to write (vt)	**escribir** (vt)	[eskri'βir]
to write down	**tomar nota**	[to'mar 'nota]

TIME. CALENDAR

T&P Books Publishing

17. Weekdays

Monday	**lunes** (m)	['lʲunes]
Tuesday	**martes** (m)	['martes]
Wednesday	**miércoles** (m)	['mjerkoles]
Thursday	**jueves** (m)	[χu'eβes]
Friday	**viernes** (m)	['bjernes]
Saturday	**sábado** (m)	['saβaðo]
Sunday	**domingo** (m)	[do'mingo]
today (adv)	**hoy** (adv)	[oj]
tomorrow (adv)	**mañana** (adv)	[ma'njana]
the day after tomorrow	**pasado mañana**	[pa'saðo ma'njana]
yesterday (adv)	**ayer** (adv)	[a'jer]
the day before yesterday	**anteayer** (adv)	[ante·a'jer]
day	**día** (m)	['dia]
working day	**día** (m) **de trabajo**	['dia de tra'βaχo]
public holiday	**día** (m) **de fiesta**	['dia de 'fjesta]
day off	**día** (m) **de descanso**	['dia de des'kanso]
weekend	**fin** (m) **de semana**	['fin de se'mana]
all day long	**todo el día**	['toðo elʲ 'dia]
the next day (adv)	**al día siguiente**	[alʲ 'dia si'ɣjente]
two days ago	**dos días atrás**	[dos 'dias a'tras]
the day before	**en vísperas** (adv)	[en 'bisperas]
daily (adj)	**diario** (adj)	['djario]
every day (adv)	**cada día** (adv)	['kaða 'dia]
week	**semana** (f)	[se'mana]
last week (adv)	**semana** (f) **pasada**	[se'mana pa'saða]
next week (adv)	**semana** (f) **que viene**	[se'mana ke 'bjene]
weekly (adj)	**semanal** (adj)	[sema'nalʲ]
every week (adv)	**cada semana** (adv)	['kaða se'mana]
twice a week	**dos veces por semana**	[dos 'beθes por se'mana]
every Tuesday	**todos los martes**	['toðos los 'martes]

18. Hours. Day and night

morning	**mañana** (f)	[ma'njana]
in the morning	**por la mañana**	[por lʲa ma'njana]
noon, midday	**mediodía** (m)	['meðjo'ðia]
in the afternoon	**por la tarde**	[por lʲa 'tarðe]
evening	**noche** (f)	['notʃe]

in the evening	**por la noche**	[por lʲa 'noʧe]
night	**noche** (f)	['noʧe]
at night	**por la noche**	[por lʲa 'noʧe]
midnight	**medianoche** (f)	['meðja'noʧe]
second	**segundo** (m)	[se'ɣundo]
minute	**minuto** (m)	[mi'nuto]
hour	**hora** (f)	['ora]
half an hour	**media hora** (f)	['meðja 'ora]
a quarter-hour	**cuarto** (m) **de hora**	[ku'arto de 'ora]
fifteen minutes	**quince minutos**	['kinθe mi'nutos]
24 hours	**veinticuatro horas**	['bejti·ku'atro 'oras]
sunrise	**salida** (f) **del sol**	[sa'liða delʲ 'solʲ]
dawn	**amanecer** (m)	[amane'θer]
early morning	**madrugada** (f)	[maðru'ɣaða]
sunset	**puesta** (f) **del sol**	[pu'esta delʲ 'solʲ]
early in the morning	**de madrugada**	[de maðru'ɣaða]
this morning	**esta mañana**	['esta ma'njana]
tomorrow morning	**mañana por la mañana**	[ma'njana por lʲa ma'njana]
this afternoon	**esta tarde**	['esta 'tarðe]
in the afternoon	**por la tarde**	[por lʲa 'tarðe]
tomorrow afternoon	**mañana por la tarde**	[ma'njana por lʲa 'tarðe]
tonight (this evening)	**esta noche**	['esta 'noʧe]
tomorrow night	**mañana por la noche**	[ma'njana por lʲa 'noʧe]
at 3 o'clock sharp	**a las tres en punto**	[a lʲas 'tres en 'punto]
about 4 o'clock	**a eso de las cuatro**	[a 'eso de lʲas ku'atro]
by 12 o'clock	**para las doce**	['para lʲas 'doθe]
in 20 minutes	**dentro de veinte minutos**	['dentro de 'bejnte mi'nutos]
in an hour	**dentro de una hora**	['dentro de 'una 'ora]
on time (adv)	**a tiempo** (adv)	[a 'tjempo]
a quarter of ...	**... menos cuarto**	['menos ku'arto]
within an hour	**durante una hora**	[du'rante 'una 'ora]
every 15 minutes	**cada quince minutos**	['kaða 'kinθe mi'nutos]
round the clock	**día y noche**	['dia i 'noʧe]

19. Months. Seasons

January	**enero** (m)	[e'nero]
February	**febrero** (m)	[fe'βrero]
March	**marzo** (m)	['marθo]
April	**abril** (m)	[a'βrilʲ]
May	**mayo** (m)	['majo]

June	**junio** (m)	['χunjo]
July	**julio** (m)	['χuljo]
August	**agosto** (m)	[a'ɣosto]
September	**septiembre** (m)	[sep'tjembre]
October	**octubre** (m)	[ok'tuβre]
November	**noviembre** (m)	[no'βjembre]
December	**diciembre** (m)	[di'θjembre]
spring	**primavera** (f)	[prima'βera]
in spring	**en primavera**	[en prima'βera]
spring (as adj)	**de primavera** (adj)	[de prima'βera]
summer	**verano** (m)	[be'rano]
in summer	**en verano**	[em be'rano]
summer (as adj)	**de verano** (adj)	[de be'rano]
fall	**otoño** (m)	[o'tonjo]
in fall	**en otoño**	[en o'tonjo]
fall (as adj)	**de otoño** (adj)	[de o'tonjo]
winter	**invierno** (m)	[im'bjerno]
in winter	**en invierno**	[en im'bjerno]
winter (as adj)	**de invierno** (adj)	[de im'bjerno]
month	**mes** (m)	[mes]
this month	**este mes**	['este 'mes]
next month	**al mes siguiente**	[alʲ 'mes si'ɣjente]
last month	**el mes pasado**	[elʲ 'mes pa'saðo]
a month ago	**hace un mes**	['aθe un 'mes]
in a month (a month later)	**dentro de un mes**	['dentro de un mes]
in 2 months (2 months later)	**dentro de dos meses**	['dentro de dos 'meses]
the whole month	**todo el mes**	['toðo elʲ 'mes]
all month long	**todo un mes**	['toðo un 'mes]
monthly (~ magazine)	**mensual** (adj)	[mensu'alʲ]
monthly (adv)	**mensualmente** (adv)	[mensualʲ'mente]
every month	**cada mes**	['kaða 'mes]
twice a month	**dos veces por mes**	[dos 'beθes por 'mes]
year	**año** (m)	['anjo]
this year	**este año**	['este 'anjo]
next year	**el próximo año**	[elʲ 'proksimo 'anjo]
last year	**el año pasado**	[elʲ 'anjo pa'saðo]
a year ago	**hace un año**	['aθe un 'anjo]
in a year	**dentro de un año**	['dentro de un 'anjo]
in two years	**dentro de dos años**	['dentro de dos 'anjos]
the whole year	**todo el año**	['toðo elʲ 'anjo]
all year long	**todo un año**	['toðo un 'anjo]
every year	**cada año**	['kaða 'anjo]

annual (adj) **anual** (adj) [anu'alʲ]
annually (adv) **anualmente** (adv) [anualʲ'mente]
4 times a year **cuatro veces por año** [ku'atro 'beθes por 'anjo]

date (e.g., today's ~) **fecha** (f) ['fetʃa]
date (e.g., ~ of birth) **fecha** (f) ['fetʃa]
calendar **calendario** (m) [kalen'darjo]

half a year **medio año** (m) ['meðjo 'anjo]
six months **seis meses** ['sejs 'meses]
season (summer, etc.) **estación** (f) [esta'θjon]
century **siglo** (m) ['siɣlo]

TRAVEL. HOTEL

T&P Books Publishing

20. Trip. Travel

tourism, travel	**turismo** (m)	[tu'rismo]
tourist	**turista** (m)	[tu'rista]
trip, voyage	**viaje** (m)	['bjaχe]
adventure	**aventura** (f)	[aβen'tura]
trip, journey	**viaje** (m)	['bjaχe]
vacation	**vacaciones** (f pl)	[baka'θjones]
to be on vacation	**estar de vacaciones**	[es'tar de baka'θjones]
rest	**descanso** (m)	[des'kanso]
train	**tren** (m)	['tren]
by train	**en tren**	[en 'tren]
airplane	**avión** (m)	[a'βjon]
by airplane	**en avión**	[en a'βjon]
by car	**en coche**	[en 'koʧe]
by ship	**en barco**	[en 'barko]
luggage	**equipaje** (m)	[eki'paχe]
suitcase	**maleta** (f)	[ma'leta]
luggage cart	**carrito** (m) **de equipaje**	[ka'rito de eki'paχe]
passport	**pasaporte** (m)	[pasa'porte]
visa	**visado** (m)	[bi'saðo]
ticket	**billete** (m)	[bi'jete]
air ticket	**billete** (m) **de avión**	[bi'jete de a'βjon]
guidebook	**guía** (f)	['gia]
map (tourist ~)	**mapa** (m)	['mapa]
area (rural ~)	**área** (m)	['area]
place, site	**lugar** (m)	[lʲu'ɣar]
exotica (n)	**exotismo** (m)	[ekso'tismo]
exotic (adj)	**exótico** (adj)	[e'ksotiko]
amazing (adj)	**asombroso** (adj)	[asom'broso]
group	**grupo** (m)	['grupo]
excursion, sightseeing tour	**excursión** (f)	[eskur'θjon]
guide (person)	**guía** (m)	['gia]

21. Hotel

hotel	**hotel** (m)	[o'telʲ]
motel	**motel** (m)	[mo'telʲ]

three-star (~ hotel)	**de tres estrellas**	[de 'tres es'trejas]
five-star	**de cinco estrellas**	[de 'θiŋko es'trejas]
to stay (in a hotel, etc.)	**hospedarse** (vr)	[ospe'ðarse]
room	**habitación** (f)	[aβita'θjon]
single room	**habitación** (f) **individual**	[aβita'θjon indiβiðu'al^j]
double room	**habitación** (f) **doble**	[aβita'θjon 'doβle]
to book a room	**reservar una habitación**	[reser'βar 'una aβita'θjon]
half board	**media pensión** (f)	['meðja pen'θjon]
full board	**pensión** (f) **completa**	[pen'θjon kom'pleta]
with bath	**con baño**	[kon 'banjo]
with shower	**con ducha**	[kon 'dutʃa]
satellite television	**televisión** (f) **satélite**	[teleβi'θjon sa'telite]
air-conditioner	**climatizador** (m)	[klimatiθa'ðor]
towel	**toalla** (f)	[to'aja]
key	**llave** (f)	['jaβe]
administrator	**administrador** (m)	[aðministra'ðor]
chambermaid	**camarera** (f)	[kama'rera]
porter, bellboy	**maletero** (m)	[male'tero]
doorman	**portero** (m)	[por'tero]
restaurant	**restaurante** (m)	[restau'rante]
pub, bar	**bar** (m)	[bar]
breakfast	**desayuno** (m)	[desa'juno]
dinner	**cena** (f)	['θena]
buffet	**buffet** (m) **libre**	[bu'fet 'liβre]
lobby	**vestíbulo** (m)	[bes'tiβulo]
elevator	**ascensor** (m)	[aθen'sor]
DO NOT DISTURB	**NO MOLESTAR**	[no moles'tar]
NO SMOKING	**PROHIBIDO FUMAR**	[proi'βiðo fu'mar]

22. Sightseeing

monument	**monumento** (m)	[monu'mento]
fortress	**fortaleza** (f)	[forta'leθa]
palace	**palacio** (m)	[pa'l^jaθjo]
castle	**castillo** (m)	[kas'tijo]
tower	**torre** (f)	['tore]
mausoleum	**mausoleo** (m)	[mauso'leo]
architecture	**arquitectura** (f)	[arkitek'tura]
medieval (adj)	**medieval** (adj)	[meðje'βal^j]
ancient (adj)	**antiguo** (adj)	[an'tiɣuo]
national (adj)	**nacional** (adj)	[naθjo'nal^j]
famous (monument, etc.)	**conocido** (adj)	[kono'θiðo]

tourist	**turista** (m)	[tu'rista]
guide (person)	**guía** (m)	['gia]
excursion, sightseeing tour	**excursión** (f)	[eskur'θjon]
to show (vt)	**mostrar** (vt)	[mos'trar]
to tell (vt)	**contar** (vt)	[kon'tar]
to find (vt)	**encontrar** (vt)	[eŋkon'trar]
to get lost (lose one's way)	**perderse** (vr)	[per'ðerse]
map (e.g., subway ~)	**plano** (m), **mapa** (m)	['plʲano], ['mapa]
map (e.g., city ~)	**mapa** (m)	['mapa]
souvenir, gift	**recuerdo** (m)	[reku'erðo]
gift shop	**tienda** (f) **de regalos**	['tjenda de re'ɣalos]
to take pictures	**hacer fotos**	[a'θer 'fotos]
to have one's picture taken	**fotografiarse** (vr)	[fotoɣra'fjarse]

TRANSPORTATION

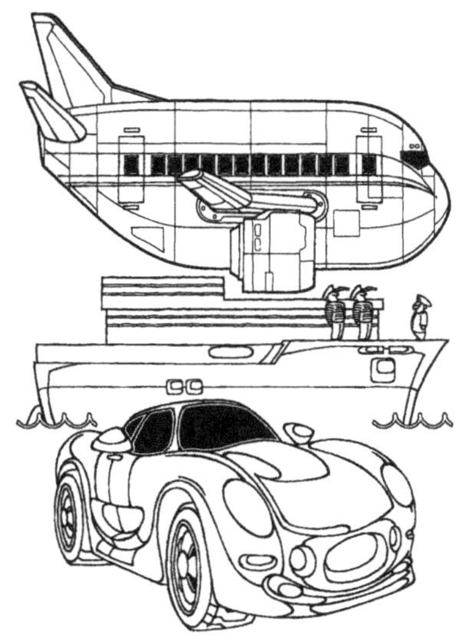

T&P Books Publishing

23. Airport

airport	**aeropuerto** (m)	[aeropu'erto]
airplane	**avión** (m)	[a'βjon]
airline	**compañía** (f) **aérea**	[kompa'njia a'erea]
air traffic controller	**controlador** (m) **aéreo**	[kontrolʲa'ðor a'ereo]
departure	**despegue** (m)	[des'peɣe]
arrival	**llegada** (f)	[je'ɣaða]
to arrive (by plane)	**llegar** (vi)	[je'ɣar]
departure time	**hora** (f) **de salida**	['ora de sa'liða]
arrival time	**hora** (f) **de llegada**	['ora de je'ɣaða]
to be delayed	**retrasarse** (vr)	[retra'sarse]
flight delay	**retraso** (m) **de vuelo**	[re'traso de bu'elo]
information board	**pantalla** (f) **de información**	[pan'taja de iɱforma'θjon]
information	**información** (f)	[iɱforma'θjon]
to announce (vt)	**anunciar** (vt)	[anun'θjar]
flight (e.g., next ~)	**vuelo** (m)	[bu'elo]
customs	**aduana** (f)	[aðu'ana]
customs officer	**aduanero** (m)	[aðua'nero]
customs declaration	**declaración** (f) **de aduana**	[deklʲara'θjon de aðu'ana]
to fill out (vt)	**rellenar** (vt)	[reje'nar]
to fill out the declaration	**rellenar la declaración**	[reje'nar lʲa deklʲara'θjon]
passport control	**control** (m) **de pasaportes**	[kon'trolʲ de pasa'portes]
luggage	**equipaje** (m)	[eki'paχe]
hand luggage	**equipaje** (m) **de mano**	[eki'paχe de 'mano]
luggage cart	**carrito** (m) **de equipaje**	[ka'rito de eki'paχe]
landing	**aterrizaje** (m)	[ateri'θaχe]
landing strip	**pista** (f) **de aterrizaje**	['pista de ateri'θaχe]
to land (vi)	**aterrizar** (vi)	[ateri'θar]
airstairs	**escaleras** (f pl)	[eska'leras]
check-in	**facturación** (f), **check-in** (m)	[faktura'θjon], [ʧek·'in]
check-in counter	**mostrador** (m) **de facturación**	[mostra'ðor de faktura'θjon]
to check-in (vi)	**hacer el check-in**	[a'θer elʲ ʧek·'in]

boarding pass	**tarjeta** (f) **de embarque**	[tar'χeta de em'barke]
departure gate	**puerta** (f) **de embarque**	[pu'erta de em'barke]
transit	**tránsito** (m)	['transito]
to wait (vt)	**esperar** (vt)	[espe'rar]
departure lounge	**zona** (f) **de preembarque**	['θona de preem'barke]
to see off	**despedir** (vt)	[despe'ðir]
to say goodbye	**despedirse** (vr)	[despe'ðirse]

24. Airplane

airplane	**avión** (m)	[a'βjon]
air ticket	**billete** (m) **de avión**	[bi'jete de a'βjon]
airline	**compañía** (f) **aérea**	[kompa'njia a'erea]
airport	**aeropuerto** (m)	[aeropu'erto]
supersonic (adj)	**supersónico** (adj)	[super'soniko]
captain	**comandante** (m)	[koman'dante]
crew	**tripulación** (f)	[tripulʲa'θjon]
pilot	**piloto** (m)	[pi'loto]
flight attendant (fem.)	**azafata** (f)	[aθa'fata]
navigator	**navegador** (m)	[naβeɣa'ðor]
wings	**alas** (f pl)	['alʲas]
tail	**cola** (f)	['kolʲa]
cockpit	**cabina** (f)	[ka'βina]
engine	**motor** (m)	[mo'tor]
undercarriage (landing gear)	**tren** (m) **de aterrizaje**	['tren de ateri'θaχe]
turbine	**turbina** (f)	[tur'βina]
propeller	**hélice** (f)	['eliθe]
black box	**caja** (f) **negra**	['kaχa 'neɣra]
yoke (control column)	**timón** (m)	[ti'mon]
fuel	**combustible** (m)	[kombus'tiβle]
safety card	**instructivo** (m) **de seguridad**	[instruk'tiβo de seɣuri'ðað]
oxygen mask	**respirador** (m) **de oxígeno**	[respira'ðor de o'ksiχeno]
uniform	**uniforme** (m)	[uni'forme]
life vest	**chaleco** (m) **salvavidas**	[ʧa'leko salʲβa'βiðas]
parachute	**paracaídas** (m)	[paraka'iðas]
takeoff	**despegue** (m)	[des'peɣe]
to take off (vi)	**despegar** (vi)	[despe'ɣar]
runway	**pista** (f) **de despegue**	['pista de des'peɣe]
visibility	**visibilidad** (f)	[bisiβili'ðað]
flight (act of flying)	**vuelo** (m)	[bu'elo]

altitude	**altura** (f)	[alʲ'tura]
air pocket	**pozo** (m) **de aire**	['poθo de 'ajre]
seat	**asiento** (m)	[a'sjento]
headphones	**auriculares** (m pl)	[auriku'lʲares]
folding tray (tray table)	**mesita** (f) **plegable**	[me'sita ple'ɣaβle]
airplane window	**ventana** (f)	[ben'tana]
aisle	**pasillo** (m)	[pa'sijo]

25. Train

train	**tren** (m)	['tren]
commuter train	**tren** (m) **eléctrico**	['tren e'lektriko]
express train	**tren** (m) **rápido**	['tren 'rapiðo]
diesel locomotive	**locomotora** (f) **diésel**	[lokomo'tora 'djeselʲ]
steam locomotive	**tren** (m) **de vapor**	['tren de ba'por]
passenger car	**coche** (m)	['kotʃe]
dining car	**coche restaurante** (m)	['kotʃe restau'rante]
rails	**rieles** (m pl)	['rjeles]
railroad	**ferrocarril** (m)	[feroka'rilʲ]
railway tie	**traviesa** (f)	[tra'βjesa]
platform (railway ~)	**plataforma** (f)	[plʲata'forma]
track (~ 1, 2, etc.)	**vía** (f)	['bia]
semaphore	**semáforo** (m)	[se'maforo]
station	**estación** (f)	[esta'θjon]
engineer (train driver)	**maquinista** (m)	[maki'nista]
porter (of luggage)	**maletero** (m)	[male'tero]
car attendant	**mozo** (m) **del vagón**	['moθo delʲ ba'ɣon]
passenger	**pasajero** (m)	[pasa'χero]
conductor (ticket inspector)	**revisor** (m)	[reβi'sor]
corridor (in train)	**corredor** (m)	[kore'ðor]
emergency brake	**freno** (m) **de urgencia**	['freno de ur'χenθja]
compartment	**compartimiento** (m)	[komparti'mjento]
berth	**litera** (f)	[li'tera]
upper berth	**litera** (f) **de arriba**	[li'tera de a'riβa]
lower berth	**litera** (f) **de abajo**	[li'tera de a'βaχo]
bed linen, bedding	**ropa** (f) **de cama**	['ropa de 'kama]
ticket	**billete** (m)	[bi'jete]
schedule	**horario** (m)	[o'rarjo]
information display	**pantalla** (f) **de información**	[pan'taja de iɱforma'θjon]
to leave, to depart	**partir** (vi)	[par'tir]

departure (of train)	**partida** (f)	[par'tiða]
to arrive (ab. train)	**llegar** (vi)	[je'ɣar]
arrival	**llegada** (f)	[je'ɣaða]
to arrive by train	**llegar en tren**	[je'ɣar en 'tren]
to get on the train	**tomar el tren**	[to'mar elʲ 'tren]
to get off the train	**bajar del tren**	[ba'χar delʲ 'tren]
train wreck	**descarrilamiento** (m)	[deskarilʲa'mjento]
to derail (vi)	**descarrilarse** (vr)	[deskari'lʲarse]
steam locomotive	**tren** (m) **de vapor**	['tren de ba'por]
stoker, fireman	**fogonero** (m)	[foɣo'nero]
firebox	**hogar** (m)	[o'ɣar]
coal	**carbón** (m)	[kar'βon]

26. Ship

ship	**buque** (m)	['buke]
vessel	**navío** (m)	[na'βio]
steamship	**buque** (m) **de vapor**	['buke de ba'por]
riverboat	**motonave** (m)	[moto'naβe]
cruise ship	**trasatlántico** (m)	[trasat'lʲantiko]
cruiser	**crucero** (m)	[kru'θero]
yacht	**yate** (m)	['jate]
tugboat	**remolcador** (m)	[remolʲka'ðor]
barge	**barcaza** (f)	[bar'kaθa]
ferry	**ferry** (m)	['feri]
sailing ship	**velero** (m)	[be'lero]
brigantine	**bergantín** (m)	[berɣan'tin]
ice breaker	**rompehielos** (m)	[rompe·'jelos]
submarine	**submarino** (m)	[suβma'rino]
boat (flat-bottomed ~)	**bote** (m)	['bote]
dinghy	**bote** (m)	['bote]
lifeboat	**bote** (m) **salvavidas**	['bote salʲβa'βiðas]
motorboat	**lancha** (f) **motora**	['lʲantʃa mo'tora]
captain	**capitán** (m)	[kapi'tan]
seaman	**marinero** (m)	[mari'nero]
sailor	**marino** (m)	[ma'rino]
crew	**tripulación** (f)	[tripulʲa'θjon]
boatswain	**contramaestre** (m)	[kontrama'estre]
ship's boy	**grumete** (m)	[gru'mete]
cook	**cocinero** (m) **de abordo**	[koθi'nero de a'βorðo]

ship's doctor	**médico** (m) **del buque**	['meðiko delʲ 'buke]
deck	**cubierta** (f)	[ku'βjerta]
mast	**mástil** (m)	['mastilʲ]
sail	**vela** (f)	['belʲa]
hold	**bodega** (f)	[bo'ðeɣa]
bow (prow)	**proa** (f)	['proa]
stern	**popa** (f)	['popa]
oar	**remo** (m)	['remo]
screw propeller	**hélice** (f)	['eliθe]
cabin	**camarote** (m)	[kama'rote]
wardroom	**comedor** (m) **de oficiales**	[kome'ðor de ofi'θjales]
engine room	**sala** (f) **de máquinas**	['salʲa de 'makinas]
bridge	**puente** (m) **de mando**	[pu'ente de 'mando]
wave (radio)	**onda** (f)	['onda]
logbook	**cuaderno** (m) **de bitácora**	[kua'ðerno de bi'takora]
spyglass	**anteojo** (m)	[ante'oχo]
bell	**campana** (f)	[kam'pana]
flag	**bandera** (f)	[ban'dera]
hawser (mooring ~)	**cabo** (m)	['kaβo]
knot (bowline, etc.)	**nudo** (m)	['nuðo]
deckrails	**pasamano** (m)	[pasa'mano]
gangway	**pasarela** (f)	[pasa'relʲa]
anchor	**ancla** (f)	['aŋklʲa]
to weigh anchor	**levar ancla**	[le'βar 'aŋklʲa]
to drop anchor	**echar ancla**	[e'ʧar 'aŋklʲa]
anchor chain	**cadena** (f) **del ancla**	[ka'ðena delʲ 'aŋklʲa]
port (harbor)	**puerto** (m)	[pu'erto]
quay, wharf	**embarcadero** (m)	[embarka'ðero]
to berth (moor)	**amarrar** (vt)	[ama'rar]
to cast off	**desamarrar** (vt)	[desama'rar]
trip, voyage	**viaje** (m)	['bjaχe]
cruise (sea trip)	**crucero** (m)	[kru'θero]
course (route)	**derrota** (f)	[de'rota]
route (itinerary)	**itinerario** (m)	[itine'rarjo]
fairway (safe water channel)	**canal** (m) **navegable**	[ka'nalʲ naβe'ɣaβle]
shallows	**bajío** (m)	[ba'χio]
to run aground	**encallar** (vi)	[eŋka'jar]
storm	**tempestad** (f)	[tempes'tað]
signal	**señal** (f)	[se'njalʲ]
to sink (vi)	**hundirse** (vr)	[un'dirse]
Man overboard!	**¡Hombre al agua!**	['ombre alʲ 'aɣua]

SOS (distress signal)	**SOS**	['ese o 'ese]
ring buoy	**aro** (m) **salvavidas**	['aro salʲβa'βiðas]

CITY

T&P Books Publishing

27. Urban transportation

bus	**autobús** (m)	[auto'βus]
streetcar	**tranvía** (m)	[tram'bia]
trolley bus	**trolebús** (m)	[trole'βus]
route (of bus, etc.)	**itinerario** (m)	[itine'rarjo]
number (e.g., bus ~)	**número** (m)	['numero]
to go by ...	**ir en ...**	[ir en]
to get on (~ the bus)	**tomar** (vt)	[to'mar]
to get off ...	**bajar del ...**	[ba'χar delʲ]
stop (e.g., bus ~)	**parada** (f)	[pa'raða]
next stop	**próxima parada** (f)	['proksima pa'raða]
terminus	**parada** (f) **final**	[pa'raða fi'nalʲ]
schedule	**horario** (m)	[o'rarjo]
to wait (vt)	**esperar** (vt)	[espe'rar]
ticket	**billete** (m)	[bi'jete]
fare	**precio** (m) **del billete**	['preθjo delʲ bi'jete]
cashier (ticket seller)	**cajero** (m)	[ka'χero]
ticket inspection	**control** (m) **de billetes**	[kon'trolʲ de bi'jetes]
ticket inspector	**cobrador** (m)	[koβra'ðor]
to be late (for ...)	**llegar tarde** (vi)	[je'ɣar 'tarðe]
to miss (~ the train, etc.)	**perder** (vt)	[per'ðer]
to be in a hurry	**tener prisa**	[te'ner 'prisa]
taxi, cab	**taxi** (m)	['taksi]
taxi driver	**taxista** (m)	[ta'ksista]
by taxi	**en taxi**	[en 'taksi]
taxi stand	**parada** (f) **de taxi**	[pa'raða de 'taksi]
to call a taxi	**llamar un taxi**	[ja'mar un 'taksi]
to take a taxi	**tomar un taxi**	[to'mar un 'taksi]
traffic	**tráfico** (m)	['trafiko]
traffic jam	**atasco** (m)	[a'tasko]
rush hour	**horas** (f pl) **de punta**	['oras de 'punta]
to park (vi)	**aparcar** (vi)	[apar'kar]
to park (vt)	**aparcar** (vt)	[apar'kar]
parking lot	**aparcamiento** (m)	[aparka'mjento]
subway	**metro** (m)	['metro]
station	**estación** (f)	[esta'θjon]
to take the subway	**ir en el metro**	[ir en elʲ 'metro]

train	**tren** (m)	['tren]
train station	**estación** (f)	[esta'θjon]

28. City. Life in the city

city, town	**ciudad** (f)	[θju'ðað]
capital city	**capital** (f)	[kapi'talʲ]
village	**aldea** (f)	[alʲ'ðea]
city map	**plano** (m) **de la ciudad**	['plʲano de lʲa θju'ðað]
downtown	**centro** (m) **de la ciudad**	['θentro de lʲa θju'ðað]
suburb	**suburbio** (m)	[su'βurβjo]
suburban (adj)	**suburbano** (adj)	[suβur'βano]
outskirts	**arrabal** (m)	[ara'βalʲ]
environs (suburbs)	**afueras** (f pl)	[afu'eras]
city block	**barrio** (m)	['barjo]
residential block (area)	**zona** (f) **de viviendas**	['θona de bi'βjendas]
traffic	**tráfico** (m)	['trafiko]
traffic lights	**semáforo** (m)	[se'maforo]
public transportation	**transporte** (m) **urbano**	[trans'porte ur'βano]
intersection	**cruce** (m)	['kruθe]
crosswalk	**paso** (m) **de peatones**	['paso de pea'tones]
pedestrian underpass	**paso** (m) **subterráneo**	['paso suβte'raneo]
to cross (~ the street)	**cruzar** (vt)	[kru'θar]
pedestrian	**peatón** (m)	[pea'ton]
sidewalk	**acera** (f)	[a'θera]
bridge	**puente** (m)	[pu'ente]
embankment (river walk)	**muelle** (m)	[mu'eje]
allée (garden walkway)	**alameda** (f)	[alʲa'meða]
park	**parque** (m)	['parke]
boulevard	**bulevar** (m)	[bule'βar]
square	**plaza** (f)	['plʲaθa]
avenue (wide street)	**avenida** (f)	[aβe'niða]
street	**calle** (f)	['kaje]
side street	**callejón** (m)	[kaje'χon]
dead end	**callejón** (m) **sin salida**	[kaje'χon sin sa'liða]
house	**casa** (f)	['kasa]
building	**edificio** (m)	[eði'fiθjo]
skyscraper	**rascacielos** (m)	[raska'θjelos]
facade	**fachada** (f)	[fa'ʧaða]
roof	**techo** (m)	['teʧo]
window	**ventana** (f)	[ben'tana]
arch	**arco** (m)	['arko]

column	**columna** (f)	[ko'lʲumna]
corner	**esquina** (f)	[es'kina]
store window	**escaparate** (f)	[eskapa'rate]
signboard (store sign, etc.)	**letrero** (m)	[le'trero]
poster	**cartel** (m)	[kar'telʲ]
advertising poster	**cartel** (m) **publicitario**	[kar'telʲ puβliθi'tarjo]
billboard	**valla** (f) **publicitaria**	['baja puβliθi'tarja]
garbage, trash	**basura** (f)	[ba'sura]
trashcan (public ~)	**cajón** (m) **de basura**	[ka'χon de ba'sura]
to litter (vi)	**tirar basura**	[ti'rar ba'sura]
garbage dump	**basurero** (m)	[basu'rero]
phone booth	**cabina** (f) **telefónica**	[ka'βina tele'fonika]
lamppost	**farola** (f)	[fa'rolʲa]
bench (park ~)	**banco** (m)	['baŋko]
police officer	**policía** (m)	[poli'θia]
police	**policía** (f)	[poli'θia]
beggar	**mendigo** (m)	[men'diɣo]
homeless (n)	**persona** (f) **sin hogar**	[per'sona sin o'ɣar]

29. Urban institutions

store	**tienda** (f)	['tjenda]
drugstore, pharmacy	**farmacia** (f)	[far'maθja]
eyeglass store	**óptica** (f)	['optika]
shopping mall	**centro** (m) **comercial**	['θentro komer'θjalʲ]
supermarket	**supermercado** (m)	[supermer'kaðo]
bakery	**panadería** (f)	[panaðe'ria]
baker	**panadero** (m)	[pana'ðero]
pastry shop	**pastelería** (f)	[pastele'ria]
grocery store	**tienda** (f) **de comestibles**	['tjenda de komes'tiβles]
butcher shop	**carnicería** (f)	[karniθe'ria]
produce store	**verdulería** (f)	[berðule'ria]
market	**mercado** (m)	[mer'kaðo]
coffee house	**cafetería** (f)	[kafete'ria]
restaurant	**restaurante** (m)	[restau'rante]
pub, bar	**cervecería** (f)	[θerβeθe'ria]
pizzeria	**pizzería** (f)	[pitse'ria]
hair salon	**peluquería** (f)	[pelʲuke'ria]
post office	**oficina** (f) **de correos**	[ofi'θina de ko'reos]
dry cleaners	**tintorería** (f)	[tintore'ria]
photo studio	**estudio** (m) **fotográfico**	[es'tuðjo foto'ɣrafiko]
shoe store	**zapatería** (f)	[θapate'ria]

bookstore	**librería** (f)	[liβre'ria]
sporting goods store	**tienda** (f) **deportiva**	['tjenda depor'tiβa]
clothes repair shop	**arreglos** (m pl) **de ropa**	[a'reɣlos de 'ropa]
formal wear rental	**alquiler** (m) **de ropa**	[alʲki'ler de 'ropa]
video rental store	**videoclub** (m)	[biðeo·'klʲuβ]
circus	**circo** (m)	['θirko]
zoo	**zoo** (m)	['θoo]
movie theater	**cine** (m)	['θine]
museum	**museo** (m)	[mu'seo]
library	**biblioteca** (f)	[biβlio'teka]
theater	**teatro** (m)	[te'atro]
opera (opera house)	**ópera** (f)	['opera]
nightclub	**club** (m) **nocturno**	[klʲuβ nok'turno]
casino	**casino** (m)	[ka'sino]
mosque	**mezquita** (f)	[meθ'kita]
synagogue	**sinagoga** (f)	[sina'ɣoɣa]
cathedral	**catedral** (f)	[kate'ðralʲ]
temple	**templo** (m)	['templo]
church	**iglesia** (f)	[i'ɣlesja]
college	**instituto** (m)	[insti'tuto]
university	**universidad** (f)	[uniβersi'ðað]
school	**escuela** (f)	[esku'elʲa]
prefecture	**prefectura** (f)	[prefek'tura]
city hall	**alcaldía** (f)	[alʲkalʲ'ðia]
hotel	**hotel** (m)	[o'telʲ]
bank	**banco** (m)	['baŋko]
embassy	**embajada** (f)	[emba'χaða]
travel agency	**agencia** (f) **de viajes**	[a'χenθja de 'bjaχes]
information office	**oficina** (f) **de información**	[ofi'θina de iɱforma'θjon]
currency exchange	**oficina** (f) **de cambio**	[ofi'θina de 'kambjo]
subway	**metro** (m)	['metro]
hospital	**hospital** (m)	[ospi'talʲ]
gas station	**gasolinera** (f)	[gasoli'nera]
parking lot	**aparcamiento** (m)	[aparka'mjento]

30. Signs

signboard (store sign, etc.)	**letrero** (m)	[le'trero]
notice (door sign, etc.)	**cartel** (m)	[kar'telʲ]
poster	**pancarta** (f)	[paŋ'karta]
direction sign	**signo** (m) **de dirección**	['siɣno de direk'θjon]

arrow (sign)	**flecha** (f)	['fleʧa]
caution	**advertencia** (f)	[aðβer'tenθja]
warning sign	**aviso** (m)	[a'βiso]
to warn (vt)	**advertir** (vt)	[aðβer'tir]
rest day (weekly ~)	**día** (m) **de descanso**	['dia de des'kanso]
timetable (schedule)	**horario** (m)	[o'rarjo]
opening hours	**horario** (m) **de apertura**	[o'rarjo de aper'tura]
WELCOME!	**¡BIENVENIDOS!**	[bjembe'niðos]
ENTRANCE	**ENTRADA**	[en'traða]
EXIT	**SALIDA**	[sa'liða]
PUSH	**EMPUJAR**	[empu'χar]
PULL	**TIRAR**	[ti'rar]
OPEN	**ABIERTO**	[a'βjerto]
CLOSED	**CERRADO**	[θe'raðo]
WOMEN	**MUJERES**	[mu'χeres]
MEN	**HOMBRES**	['ombres]
DISCOUNTS	**REBAJAS**	[re'βaχas]
SALE	**SALDOS**	['salʲðos]
NEW!	**NOVEDAD**	[noβe'ðað]
FREE	**GRATIS**	['gratis]
ATTENTION!	**¡ATENCIÓN!**	[aten'θjon]
NO VACANCIES	**COMPLETO**	[kom'pleto]
RESERVED	**RESERVADO**	[reser'βaðo]
ADMINISTRATION	**ADMINISTRACIÓN**	[aðministra'θjon]
STAFF ONLY	**SÓLO PERSONAL AUTORIZADO**	['solo perso'nalʲ autori'θaðo]
BEWARE OF THE DOG!	**CUIDADO CON EL PERRO**	[kui'ðaðo kon elʲ 'pero]
NO SMOKING	**PROHIBIDO FUMAR**	[proi'βiðo fu'mar]
DO NOT TOUCH!	**NO TOCAR**	[no to'kar]
DANGEROUS	**PELIGROSO**	[peli'ɣroso]
DANGER	**PELIGRO**	[pe'liɣro]
HIGH VOLTAGE	**ALTA TENSIÓN**	['alʲta ten'sjon]
NO SWIMMING!	**PROHIBIDO BAÑARSE**	[proi'βiðo ba'njarse]
OUT OF ORDER	**NO FUNCIONA**	[no fun'θjona]
FLAMMABLE	**INFLAMABLE**	[iɱflʲa'maβle]
FORBIDDEN	**PROHIBIDO**	[proi'βiðo]
NO TRESPASSING!	**PROHIBIDO EL PASO**	[proi'βiðo elʲ 'paso]
WET PAINT	**RECIÉN PINTADO**	[re'θjen pin'taðo]

31. Shopping

to buy (purchase)	**comprar** (vt)	[kom'prar]
purchase	**compra** (f)	['kompra]
to go shopping	**hacer compras**	[a'θer 'kompras]
shopping	**compras** (f pl)	['kompras]
to be open (ab. store)	**estar abierto**	[es'tar a'βjerto]
to be closed	**estar cerrado**	[es'tar θe'raðo]
footwear, shoes	**calzado** (m)	[kalʲ'θaðo]
clothes, clothing	**ropa** (f), **vestido** (m)	['ropa], [bes'tiðo]
cosmetics	**cosméticos** (m pl)	[kos'metikos]
food products	**productos alimenticios**	[pro'ðuktos alimen'tiθjos]
gift, present	**regalo** (m)	[re'ɣalo]
salesman	**vendedor** (m)	[bende'ðor]
saleswoman	**vendedora** (f)	[bende'ðora]
check out, cash desk	**caja** (f)	['kaχa]
mirror	**espejo** (m)	[es'peχo]
counter (store ~)	**mostrador** (m)	[mostra'ðor]
fitting room	**probador** (m)	[proβa'ðor]
to try on	**probar** (vt)	[pro'βar]
to fit (ab. dress, etc.)	**quedar** (vi)	[ke'ðar]
to like (I like ...)	**gustar** (vi)	[gus'tar]
price	**precio** (m)	['preθjo]
price tag	**etiqueta** (f) **de precio**	[eti'keta de 'preθjo]
to cost (vt)	**costar** (vt)	[kos'tar]
How much?	**¿cuánto?**	[ku'anto]
discount	**descuento** (m)	[desku'ento]
inexpensive (adj)	**no costoso** (adj)	[no kos'toso]
cheap (adj)	**barato** (adj)	[ba'rato]
expensive (adj)	**caro** (adj)	['karo]
It's expensive	**Es caro**	[es 'karo]
rental (n)	**alquiler** (m)	[alʲki'ler]
to rent (~ a tuxedo)	**alquilar** (vt)	[alʲki'lʲar]
credit (trade credit)	**crédito** (m)	['kreðito]
on credit (adv)	**a crédito** (adv)	[a 'kreðito]

CLOTHING & ACCESSORIES

T&P Books Publishing

32. Outerwear. Coats

clothes	**ropa** (f), **vestido** (m)	['ropa], [bes'tiðo]
outerwear	**ropa** (f) **de calle**	['ropa de 'kaje]
winter clothing	**ropa** (f) **de invierno**	['ropa de im'bjerno]
coat (overcoat)	**abrigo** (m)	[a'βriɣo]
fur coat	**abrigo** (m) **de piel**	[a'βriɣo de pjelʲ]
fur jacket	**abrigo** (m) **corto de piel**	[a'βriɣo 'korto de pjelʲ]
down coat	**chaqueta plumón** (m)	[ʧa'keta plʲu'mon]
jacket (e.g., leather ~)	**cazadora** (f)	[kaθa'ðora]
raincoat (trenchcoat, etc.)	**impermeable** (m)	[imperme'aβle]
waterproof (adj)	**impermeable** (adj)	[imperme'aβle]

33. Men's & women's clothing

shirt (button shirt)	**camisa** (f)	[ka'misa]
pants	**pantalones** (m pl)	[panta'lones]
jeans	**vaqueros** (m pl)	[ba'keros]
suit jacket	**chaqueta** (f), **saco** (m)	[ʧa'keta], ['sako]
suit	**traje** (m)	['traχe]
dress (frock)	**vestido** (m)	[bes'tiðo]
skirt	**falda** (f)	['falʲða]
blouse	**blusa** (f)	['blʲusa]
knitted jacket (cardigan, etc.)	**rebeca** (f), **chaqueta** (f) **de punto**	[re'βeka], [ʧa'keta de 'punto]
jacket (of woman's suit)	**chaqueta** (f)	[ʧa'keta]
T-shirt	**camiseta** (f)	[kami'seta]
shorts (short trousers)	**shorts** (m pl)	['ʃorts]
tracksuit	**traje** (m) **deportivo**	['traχe depor'tiβo]
bathrobe	**bata** (f) **de baño**	['bata de 'banjo]
pajamas	**pijama** (f)	[pi'χama]
sweater	**jersey** (m), **suéter** (m)	[χer'sej], [su'eter]
pullover	**pulóver** (m)	[pu'loβer]
vest	**chaleco** (m)	[ʧa'leko]
tailcoat	**frac** (m)	[frak]
tuxedo	**esmoquin** (m)	[es'mokin]
uniform	**uniforme** (m)	[uni'forme]
workwear	**ropa** (f) **de trabajo**	['ropa de tra'βaχo]

overalls	**mono** (m)	['mono]
coat (e.g., doctor's smock)	**bata** (f)	['bata]

34. Clothing. Underwear

underwear	**ropa** (f) **interior**	['ropa inte'rjor]
undershirt (A-shirt)	**camiseta** (f) **interior**	[kami'θeta inte'rjor]
socks	**calcetines** (m pl)	[kalʲθe'tines]
nightgown	**camisón** (m)	[kami'son]
bra	**sostén** (m)	[sos'ten]
knee highs (knee-high socks)	**calcetines** (m pl) **altos**	[kalʲθe'tines 'alʲtos]
pantyhose	**pantimedias** (f pl)	[panti'meðjas]
stockings (thigh highs)	**medias** (f pl)	['meðjas]
bathing suit	**traje** (m) **de baño**	['traχe de 'banjo]

35. Headwear

hat	**gorro** (m)	['goro]
fedora	**sombrero** (m)	[som'brero]
baseball cap	**gorra** (f) **de béisbol**	['gora de 'bejsβolʲ]
flatcap	**gorra** (f) **plana**	['gora 'plʲana]
beret	**boina** (f)	['bojna]
hood	**capuchón** (m)	[kapu'ʧon]
panama hat	**panamá** (m)	[pana'ma]
knit cap (knitted hat)	**gorro** (m) **de punto**	['goro de 'punto]
headscarf	**pañuelo** (m)	[panju'elo]
women's hat	**sombrero** (m) **de mujer**	[som'brero de mu'χer]
hard hat	**casco** (m)	['kasko]
garrison cap	**gorro** (m) **de campaña**	['goro de kam'panja]
helmet	**casco** (m)	['kasko]
derby	**bombín** (m)	[bom'bin]
top hat	**sombrero** (m) **de copa**	[som'brero de 'kopa]

36. Footwear

footwear	**calzado** (m)	[kalʲ'θaðo]
shoes (men's shoes)	**botas** (f pl)	['botas]
shoes (women's shoes)	**zapatos** (m pl)	[θa'patos]
boots (e.g., cowboy ~)	**botas** (f pl)	['botas]
slippers	**zapatillas** (f pl)	[θapa'tijas]

tennis shoes (e.g., Nike ~)	**tenis** (m pl)	['tenis]
sneakers (e.g., Converse ~)	**zapatillas** (f pl) **de lona**	[θapa'tijas de 'lona]
sandals	**sandalias** (f pl)	[san'daljas]
cobbler (shoe repairer)	**zapatero** (m)	[θapa'tero]
heel	**tacón** (m)	[ta'kon]
pair (of shoes)	**par** (m)	[par]
shoestring	**cordón** (m)	[kor'ðon]
to lace (vt)	**encordonar** (vt)	[eŋkorðo'nar]
shoehorn	**calzador** (m)	[kalʲθa'ðor]
shoe polish	**betún** (m)	[be'tun]

37. Personal accessories

gloves	**guantes** (m pl)	[gu'antes]
mittens	**manoplas** (f pl)	[ma'noplʲas]
scarf (muffler)	**bufanda** (f)	[bu'fanda]
glasses (eyeglasses)	**gafas** (f pl)	['gafas]
frame (eyeglass ~)	**montura** (f)	[mon'tura]
umbrella	**paraguas** (m)	[pa'raɣuas]
walking stick	**bastón** (m)	[bas'ton]
hairbrush	**cepillo** (m) **de pelo**	[θe'pijo de 'pelo]
fan	**abanico** (m)	[aβa'niko]
tie (necktie)	**corbata** (f)	[kor'βata]
bow tie	**pajarita** (f)	[paχa'rita]
suspenders	**tirantes** (m pl)	[ti'rantes]
handkerchief	**moquero** (m)	[mo'kero]
comb	**peine** (m)	['pejne]
barrette	**pasador** (m) **de pelo**	[pasa'ðor de 'pelo]
hairpin	**horquilla** (f)	[or'kija]
buckle	**hebilla** (f)	[e'βija]
belt	**cinturón** (m)	[θintu'ron]
shoulder strap	**correa** (f)	[ko'rea]
bag (handbag)	**bolsa** (f)	['bolʲsa]
purse	**bolso** (m)	['bolʲso]
backpack	**mochila** (f)	[mo'ʧilʲa]

38. Clothing. Miscellaneous

fashion	**moda** (f)	['moða]
in vogue (adj)	**de moda** (adj)	[de 'moða]

fashion designer	**diseñador** (m) **de moda**	[disenja'ðor de 'moða]
collar	**cuello** (m)	[ku'ejo]
pocket	**bolsillo** (m)	[bolʲ'sijo]
pocket (as adj)	**de bolsillo** (adj)	[de bolʲ'sijo]
sleeve	**manga** (f)	['manga]
hanging loop	**presilla** (f)	[pre'sija]
fly (on trousers)	**bragueta** (f)	[bra'ɣeta]
zipper (fastener)	**cremallera** (f)	[krema'jera]
fastener	**cierre** (m)	['θjere]
button	**botón** (m)	[bo'ton]
buttonhole	**ojal** (m)	[o'χalʲ]
to come off (ab. button)	**saltar** (vi)	[salʲ'tar]
to sew (vi, vt)	**coser** (vi, vt)	[ko'ser]
to embroider (vi, vt)	**bordar** (vt)	[bor'ðar]
embroidery	**bordado** (m)	[bor'ðaðo]
sewing needle	**aguja** (f)	[a'ɣuχa]
thread	**hilo** (m)	['ilo]
seam	**costura** (f)	[kos'tura]
to get dirty (vi)	**ensuciarse** (vr)	[ensu'θjarse]
stain (mark, spot)	**mancha** (f)	['manʧa]
to crease, crumple (vi)	**arrugarse** (vr)	[aru'ɣarse]
to tear, to rip (vt)	**rasgar** (vt)	[ras'ɣar]
clothes moth	**polilla** (f)	[po'lija]

39. Personal care. Cosmetics

toothpaste	**pasta** (f) **de dientes**	['pasta de 'djentes]
toothbrush	**cepillo** (m) **de dientes**	[θe'pijo de 'djentes]
to brush one's teeth	**limpiarse los dientes**	[lim'pjarse los 'djentes]
razor	**maquinilla** (f) **de afeitar**	[maki'nija de afej'tar]
shaving cream	**crema** (f) **de afeitar**	['krema de afej'tar]
to shave (vi)	**afeitarse** (vr)	[afej'tarse]
soap	**jabón** (m)	[χa'βon]
shampoo	**champú** (m)	[ʧam'pu]
scissors	**tijeras** (f pl)	[ti'χeras]
nail file	**lima** (f) **de uñas**	['lima de 'unjas]
nail clippers	**cortaúñas** (m pl)	[korta·'unjas]
tweezers	**pinzas** (f pl)	['pinθas]
cosmetics	**cosméticos** (m pl)	[kos'metikos]
face mask	**mascarilla** (f)	[maska'rija]
manicure	**manicura** (f)	[mani'kura]
to have a manicure	**hacer la manicura**	[a'θer lʲa mani'kura]
pedicure	**pedicura** (f)	[peði'kura]

make-up bag	**bolsa** (f) **de maquillaje**	['bolʲsa de maki'jaχe]
face powder	**polvos** (m pl)	['polʲβos]
powder compact	**polvera** (f)	[polʲ'βera]
blusher	**colorete** (m)	[kolo'rete]
perfume (bottled)	**perfume** (m)	[per'fume]
toilet water (lotion)	**eau de toilette** (f)	[o de tua'let]
lotion	**loción** (f)	[lo'θjon]
cologne	**agua** (f) **de colonia**	['aɣua de ko'lonja]
eyeshadow	**sombra** (f) **de ojos**	['sombra de 'oχos]
eyeliner	**lápiz** (m) **de ojos**	['lʲapiθ de 'oχos]
mascara	**rímel** (m)	['rimelʲ]
lipstick	**pintalabios** (m)	[pinta·'lʲaβios]
nail polish, enamel	**esmalte** (m) **de uñas**	[es'malʲte de 'unjas]
hair spray	**fijador** (m) **(para el pelo)**	[fiχa'ðor]
deodorant	**desodorante** (m)	[desoðo'rante]
cream	**crema** (f)	['krema]
face cream	**crema** (f) **de belleza**	['krema de be'jeθa]
hand cream	**crema** (f) **de manos**	['krema de 'manos]
anti-wrinkle cream	**crema** (f) **antiarrugas**	['krema anti·a'ruɣas]
day (as adj)	**de día** (adj)	[de 'dia]
night (as adj)	**de noche** (adj)	[de 'noʧe]
tampon	**tampón** (m)	[tam'pon]
toilet paper (toilet roll)	**papel** (m) **higiénico**	[pa'pelʲ i'χjeniko]
hair dryer	**secador** (m) **de pelo**	[seka'ðor de 'pelo]

40. Watches. Clocks

watch (wristwatch)	**reloj** (m)	[re'loχ]
dial	**esfera** (f)	[es'fera]
hand (of clock, watch)	**aguja** (f)	[a'ɣuχa]
metal watch band	**pulsera** (f)	[pulʲ'sera]
watch strap	**correa** (f)	[ko'rea]
battery	**pila** (f)	['pilʲa]
to be dead (battery)	**descargarse** (vr)	[deskar'ɣarse]
to change a battery	**cambiar la pila**	[kam'bjar lʲa 'pilʲa]
to run fast	**adelantarse** (vr)	[aðelʲan'tarθe]
to run slow	**retrasarse** (vr)	[retra'sarse]
wall clock	**reloj** (m) **de pared**	[re'loχ de pa'reð]
hourglass	**reloj** (m) **de arena**	[re'loχ de a'rena]
sundial	**reloj** (m) **de sol**	[re'loχ de 'solʲ]
alarm clock	**despertador** (m)	[desperta'ðor]
watchmaker	**relojero** (m)	[relo'χero]
to repair (vt)	**reparar** (vt)	[repa'rar]

EVERYDAY EXPERIENCE

T&P Books Publishing

41. Money

money	**dinero** (m)	[di'nero]
currency exchange	**cambio** (m)	['kambjo]
exchange rate	**curso** (m)	['kurso]
ATM	**cajero** (m) **automático**	[ka'χero auto'matiko]
coin	**moneda** (f)	[mo'neða]
dollar	**dólar** (m)	['dolʲar]
euro	**euro** (m)	['euro]
lira	**lira** (f)	['lira]
Deutschmark	**marco** (m) **alemán**	['marko ale'man]
franc	**franco** (m)	['fraŋko]
pound sterling	**libra esterlina** (f)	['liβra ester'lina]
yen	**yen** (m)	[jen]
debt	**deuda** (f)	['deuða]
debtor	**deudor** (m)	[deu'ðor]
to lend (money)	**prestar** (vt)	[pres'tar]
to borrow (vi, vt)	**tomar prestado**	[to'mar pres'taðo]
bank	**banco** (m)	['baŋko]
account	**cuenta** (f)	[ku'enta]
to deposit into the account	**ingresar en la cuenta**	[ingre'sar en lʲa ku'enta]
to withdraw (vt)	**sacar de la cuenta**	[sa'kar de lʲa ku'enta]
credit card	**tarjeta** (f) **de crédito**	[tar'χeta de 'kreðito]
cash	**dinero** (m) **en efectivo**	[di'nero en efek'tiβo]
check	**cheque** (m)	['ʧeke]
to write a check	**sacar un cheque**	[sa'kar un 'ʧeke]
checkbook	**talonario** (m)	[talo'narjo]
wallet	**cartera** (f)	[kar'tera]
change purse	**monedero** (m)	[mone'ðero]
safe	**caja** (f) **fuerte**	['kaχa fu'erte]
heir	**heredero** (m)	[ere'ðero]
inheritance	**herencia** (f)	[e'renθja]
fortune (wealth)	**fortuna** (f)	[for'tuna]
lease	**arriendo** (m)	[a'rjendo]
rent (money)	**alquiler** (m)	[alʲki'ler]
to rent (sth from sb)	**alquilar** (vt)	[alʲki'lʲar]
price	**precio** (m)	['preθjo]
cost	**coste** (m)	['koste]

sum	**suma** (f)	['suma]
to spend (vt)	**gastar** (vt)	[gas'tar]
expenses	**gastos** (m pl)	['gastos]
to economize (vi, vt)	**economizar** (vi, vt)	[ekonomi'θar]
economical	**económico** (adj)	[eko'nomiko]
to pay (vi, vt)	**pagar** (vi, vt)	[pa'ɣar]
payment	**pago** (m)	['paɣo]
change (give the ~)	**cambio** (m)	['kambjo]
tax	**impuesto** (m)	[impu'esto]
fine	**multa** (f)	['mulʲta]
to fine (vt)	**multar** (vt)	[mulʲ'tar]

42. Post. Postal service

post office	**oficina** (f) **de correos**	[ofi'θina de ko'reos]
mail (letters, etc.)	**correo** (m)	[ko'reo]
mailman	**cartero** (m)	[kar'tero]
opening hours	**horario** (m) **de apertura**	[o'rarjo de aper'tura]
letter	**carta** (f)	['karta]
registered letter	**carta** (f) **certificada**	['karta θertifi'kaðа]
postcard	**tarjeta** (f) **postal**	[tar'χeta pos'talʲ]
telegram	**telegrama** (m)	[tele'ɣrama]
package (parcel)	**paquete** (m) **postal**	[pa'kete pos'talʲ]
money transfer	**giro** (m) **postal**	['χiro pos'talʲ]
to receive (vt)	**recibir** (vt)	[reθi'βir]
to send (vt)	**enviar** (vt)	[em'bjar]
sending	**envío** (m)	[em'bio]
address	**dirección** (f)	[direk'θjon]
ZIP code	**código** (m) **postal**	['koðiɣo pos'talʲ]
sender	**expedidor** (m)	[ekspeði'ðor]
receiver	**destinatario** (m)	[destina'tarjo]
name (first name)	**nombre** (m)	['nombre]
surname (last name)	**apellido** (m)	[ape'jiðo]
postage rate	**tarifa** (f)	[ta'rifa]
standard (adj)	**ordinario** (adj)	[orði'narjo]
economical (adj)	**económico** (adj)	[eko'nomiko]
weight	**peso** (m)	['peso]
to weigh (~ letters)	**pesar** (vt)	[pe'sar]
envelope	**sobre** (m)	['soβre]
postage stamp	**sello** (m)	['sejo]
to stamp an envelope	**poner un sello**	[po'ner un 'sejo]

43. Banking

bank	**banco** (m)	['baŋko]
branch (of bank, etc.)	**sucursal** (f)	[sukur'salʲ]
bank clerk, consultant	**asesor** (m)	[ase'sor]
manager (director)	**gerente** (m)	[χe'rente]
bank account	**cuenta** (f)	[ku'enta]
account number	**numero** (m) **de la cuenta**	['numero de lʲa ku'enta]
checking account	**cuenta** (f) **corriente**	[ku'enta ko'rjente]
savings account	**cuenta** (f) **de ahorros**	[ku'enta de a'oros]
to open an account	**abrir una cuenta**	[a'βrir una ku'enta]
to close the account	**cerrar la cuenta**	[θe'rar lʲa ku'enta]
to deposit into the account	**ingresar en la cuenta**	[ingre'sar en lʲa ku'enta]
to withdraw (vt)	**sacar de la cuenta**	[sa'kar de lʲa ku'enta]
deposit	**depósito** (m)	[de'posito]
to make a deposit	**hacer un depósito**	[a'θer un de'posito]
wire transfer	**giro** (m)	['χiro]
to wire, to transfer	**hacer un giro**	[a'θer un 'χiro]
sum	**suma** (f)	['suma]
How much?	**¿Cuánto?**	[ku'anto]
signature	**firma** (f)	['firma]
to sign (vt)	**firmar** (vt)	[fir'mar]
credit card	**tarjeta** (f) **de crédito**	[tar'χeta de 'kreðito]
code (PIN code)	**código** (m)	['koðiɣo]
credit card number	**número** (m) **de tarjeta de crédito**	['numero de tar'χeta de 'kreðito]
ATM	**cajero** (m) **automático**	[ka'χero auto'matiko]
check	**cheque** (m)	['ʧeke]
to write a check	**sacar un cheque**	[sa'kar un 'ʧeke]
checkbook	**talonario** (m)	[talo'narjo]
loan (bank ~)	**crédito** (m)	['kreðito]
to apply for a loan	**pedir el crédito**	[pe'ðir elʲ 'kreðito]
to get a loan	**obtener un crédito**	[oβte'ner un 'kreðito]
to give a loan	**conceder un crédito**	[konθe'ðer un 'kreðito]
guarantee	**garantía** (f)	[garan'tia]

44. Telephone. Phone conversation

telephone	**teléfono** (m)	[te'lefono]
cell phone	**teléfono** (m) **móvil**	[te'lefono 'moβilʲ]

answering machine	**contestador** (m)	[kontesta'ðor]
to call (by phone)	**llamar, telefonear**	[ja'mar], [telefone'ar]
phone call	**llamada** (f)	[ja'maða]
to dial a number	**marcar un número**	[mar'kar un 'numero]
Hello!	**¿Sí?, ¿Dígame?**	[si], ['diɣame]
to ask (vt)	**preguntar** (vt)	[preɣun'tar]
to answer (vi, vt)	**responder** (vi, vt)	[respon'der]
to hear (vt)	**oír** (vt)	[o'ir]
well (adv)	**bien** (adv)	[bjen]
not well (adv)	**mal** (adv)	[malʲ]
noises (interference)	**ruidos** (m pl)	[ru'iðos]
receiver	**auricular** (m)	[auriku'lʲar]
busy (engaged)	**ocupado** (adj)	[oku'paðo]
to ring (ab. phone)	**sonar** (vi)	[so'nar]
telephone book	**guía** (f) **de teléfonos**	['gia de te'lefonos]
local (adj)	**local** (adj)	[lo'kalʲ]
local call	**llamada** (f) **local**	[ja'maða lo'kalʲ]
long distance (~ call)	**de larga distancia**	[de 'larɣa dis'tanθja]
long-distance call	**llamada** (f) **interurbana**	[ja'maða interur'βana]
international (adj)	**internacional** (adj)	[internaθjo'nalʲ]
international call	**llamada** (f) **internacional**	[ja'maða internaθjo'nalʲ]

45. Cell phone

cell phone	**teléfono** (m) **móvil**	[te'lefono 'moβilʲ]
display	**pantalla** (f)	[pan'taja]
button	**botón** (m)	[bo'ton]
SIM card	**tarjeta SIM** (f)	[tar'χeta sim]
battery	**pila** (f)	['pilʲa]
to be dead (battery)	**descargarse** (vr)	[deskar'ɣarse]
charger	**cargador** (m)	[karɣa'ðor]
menu	**menú** (m)	[me'nu]
settings	**preferencias** (f pl)	[prefe'renθjas]
tune (melody)	**melodía** (f)	[melo'ðia]
to select (vt)	**seleccionar** (vt)	[selekθjo'nar]
calculator	**calculadora** (f)	[kalʲkulʲa'ðora]
voice mail	**contestador** (m)	[kontesta'ðor]
alarm clock	**despertador** (m)	[desperta'ðor]
contacts	**contactos** (m pl)	[kon'taktos]
SMS (text message)	**mensaje** (m) **de texto**	[men'saχe de 'teksto]
subscriber	**abonado** (m)	[aβo'naðo]

46. Stationery

ballpoint pen	**bolígrafo** (m)	[bo'liɣrafo]
fountain pen	**pluma** (f) **estilográfica**	['plʲuma estilo'ɣrafika]
pencil	**lápiz** (f)	['lʲapiθ]
highlighter	**marcador** (m)	[marka'ðor]
felt-tip pen	**rotulador** (m)	[rotulʲa'ðor]
notepad	**bloc** (m) **de notas**	['blok de 'notas]
agenda (diary)	**agenda** (f)	[a'χenda]
ruler	**regla** (f)	['reɣlʲa]
calculator	**calculadora** (f)	[kalʲkulʲa'ðora]
eraser	**goma** (f) **de borrar**	['goma de bo'rar]
thumbtack	**chincheta** (f)	[ʧin'ʧeta]
paper clip	**clip** (m)	[klip]
glue	**cola** (f), **pegamento** (m)	['kolʲa], [peɣa'mento]
stapler	**grapadora** (f)	[grapa'ðora]
hole punch	**perforador** (m)	[perfora'ðor]
pencil sharpener	**sacapuntas** (m)	[saka'puntas]

47. Foreign languages

language	**lengua** (f)	['lengua]
foreign (adj)	**extranjero** (adj)	[ekstran'χero]
to study (vt)	**estudiar** (vt)	[estu'ðjar]
to learn (language, etc.)	**aprender** (vt)	[apren'der]
to read (vi, vt)	**leer** (vi, vt)	[le'er]
to speak (vi, vt)	**hablar** (vi, vt)	[a'βlʲar]
to understand (vt)	**comprender** (vt)	[kompren'der]
to write (vt)	**escribir** (vt)	[eskri'βir]
fast (adv)	**rápidamente** (adv)	['rapiða'mente]
slowly (adv)	**lentamente** (adv)	[lenta'mente]
fluently (adv)	**con fluidez** (adv)	[kon flʲui'ðeθ]
rules	**reglas** (f pl)	['reɣlʲas]
grammar	**gramática** (f)	[gra'matika]
vocabulary	**vocabulario** (m)	[bokaβu'larjo]
phonetics	**fonética** (f)	[fo'netika]
textbook	**manual** (m)	[manu'alʲ]
dictionary	**diccionario** (m)	[dikθjo'narjo]
teach-yourself book	**manual** (m) **autodidáctico**	[manu'alʲ autoði'ðaktiko]
phrasebook	**guía** (f) **de conversación**	['gia de kombersa'θjon]
cassette, tape	**casete** (m)	[ka'sete]

videotape	**videocasete** (f)	[biðeo·ka'sete]
CD, compact disc	**disco compacto** (m)	['disko kom'pakto]
DVD	**DVD** (m)	[deβe'de]
alphabet	**alfabeto** (m)	[alʲfa'βeto]
to spell (vt)	**deletrear** (vt)	[deletre'ar]
pronunciation	**pronunciación** (f)	[pronunθja'θjon]
accent	**acento** (m)	[a'θento]
with an accent	**con acento**	[kon a'θento]
without an accent	**sin acento**	[sin a'θento]
word	**palabra** (f)	[pa'lʲaβra]
meaning	**significado** (m)	[siɣnifi'kaðo]
course (e.g., a French ~)	**cursos** (m pl)	['kursos]
to sign up	**inscribirse** (vr)	[inskri'βirse]
teacher	**profesor** (m)	[profe'sor]
translation (process)	**traducción** (f)	[traðuk'θjon]
translation (text, etc.)	**traducción** (f)	[traðuk'θjon]
translator	**traductor** (m)	[traðuk'tor]
interpreter	**intérprete** (m)	[in'terprete]
polyglot	**políglota** (m)	[po'liɣlota]
memory	**memoria** (f)	[me'morja]

MEALS. RESTAURANT

T&P Books Publishing

48. Table setting

spoon	**cuchara** (f)	[ku'ʧara]
knife	**cuchillo** (m)	[ku'ʧijo]
fork	**tenedor** (m)	[tene'ðor]
cup (e.g., coffee ~)	**taza** (f)	['taθa]
plate (dinner ~)	**plato** (m)	['plʲato]
saucer	**platillo** (m)	[plʲa'tijo]
napkin (on table)	**servilleta** (f)	[serβi'jeta]
toothpick	**mondadientes** (m)	[monda'ðjentes]

49. Restaurant

restaurant	**restaurante** (m)	[restau'rante]
coffee house	**cafetería** (f)	[kafete'ria]
pub, bar	**bar** (m)	[bar]
tearoom	**salón** (m) **de té**	[sa'lon de 'te]
waiter	**camarero** (m)	[kama'rero]
waitress	**camarera** (f)	[kama'rera]
bartender	**barman** (m)	['barman]
menu	**carta** (f), **menú** (m)	['karta], [me'nu]
wine list	**carta** (f) **de vinos**	['karta de 'binos]
to book a table	**reservar una mesa**	[reser'βar 'una 'mesa]
course, dish	**plato** (m)	['plʲato]
to order (meal)	**pedir** (vt)	[pe'ðir]
to make an order	**hacer el pedido**	[a'θer elʲ pe'ðiðo]
aperitif	**aperitivo** (m)	[aperi'tiβo]
appetizer	**entremés** (m)	[entre'mes]
dessert	**postre** (m)	['postre]
check	**cuenta** (f)	[ku'enta]
to pay the check	**pagar la cuenta**	[pa'ɣar lʲa ku'enta]
to give change	**dar la vuelta**	['dar lʲa bu'elta]
tip	**propina** (f)	[pro'pina]

50. Meals

food	**comida** (f)	[ko'miða]
to eat (vi, vt)	**comer** (vi, vt)	[ko'mer]

breakfast	**desayuno** (m)	[desa'juno]
to have breakfast	**desayunar** (vi)	[desaju'nar]
lunch	**almuerzo** (m)	[alʲmu'erθo]
to have lunch	**almorzar** (vi)	[alʲmor'θar]
dinner	**cena** (f)	['θena]
to have dinner	**cenar** (vi)	[θe'nar]
appetite	**apetito** (m)	[ape'tito]
Enjoy your meal!	**¡Que aproveche!**	[ke apro'βetʃe]
to open (~ a bottle)	**abrir** (vt)	[a'βrir]
to spill (liquid)	**derramar** (vt)	[dera'mar]
to spill out (vi)	**derramarse** (vr)	[dera'marse]
to boil (vi)	**hervir** (vi)	[er'βir]
to boil (vt)	**hervir** (vt)	[er'βir]
boiled (~ water)	**hervido** (adj)	[er'βiðo]
to chill, cool down (vt)	**enfriar** (vt)	[eɱfri'ar]
to chill (vi)	**enfriarse** (vr)	[eɱfri'arse]
taste, flavor	**sabor** (m)	[sa'βor]
aftertaste	**regusto** (m)	[re'ɣusto]
to slim down (lose weight)	**adelgazar** (vi)	[aðelʲɣa'θar]
diet	**dieta** (f)	[di'eta]
vitamin	**vitamina** (f)	[bita'mina]
calorie	**caloría** (f)	[kalo'ria]
vegetarian (n)	**vegetariano** (m)	[beχeta'rjano]
vegetarian (adj)	**vegetariano** (adj)	[beχeta'rjano]
fats (nutrient)	**grasas** (f pl)	['grasas]
proteins	**proteínas** (f pl)	[prote'inas]
carbohydrates	**carbohidratos** (m pl)	[karβoi'ðratos]
slice (of lemon, ham)	**loncha** (f)	['lonχa]
piece (of cake, pie)	**pedazo** (m)	[pe'ðaθo]
crumb (of bread, cake, etc.)	**miga** (f)	['miɣa]

51. Cooked dishes

course, dish	**plato** (m)	['plʲato]
cuisine	**cocina** (f)	[ko'θina]
recipe	**receta** (f)	[re'θeta]
portion	**porción** (f)	[por'θjon]
salad	**ensalada** (f)	[ensa'lʲaða]
soup	**sopa** (f)	['sopa]
clear soup (broth)	**caldo** (m)	['kalʲðo]
sandwich (bread)	**bocadillo** (m)	[boka'ðijo]

fried eggs	**huevos** (m pl) **fritos**	[u'eβos 'fritos]
hamburger (beefburger)	**hamburguesa** (f)	[ambur'ɣesa]
beefsteak	**bistec** (m)	[bis'tek]
side dish	**guarnición** (f)	[guarni'θjon]
spaghetti	**espagueti** (m)	[espa'ɣeti]
mashed potatoes	**puré** (m) **de patatas**	[pu're de pa'tatas]
pizza	**pizza** (f)	['pitsa]
porridge (oatmeal, etc.)	**gachas** (f pl)	['gatʃas]
omelet	**tortilla** (f) **francesa**	[tor'tija fran'θesa]
boiled (e.g., ~ beef)	**cocido en agua** (adj)	[ko'θiðo en 'aɣua]
smoked (adj)	**ahumado** (adj)	[au'maðo]
fried (adj)	**frito** (adj)	['frito]
dried (adj)	**seco** (adj)	['seko]
frozen (adj)	**congelado** (adj)	[konχe'lʲaðo]
pickled (adj)	**marinado** (adj)	[mari'naðo]
sweet (sugary)	**azucarado, dulce** (adj)	[aθuka'raðo], ['dulʲθe]
salty (adj)	**salado** (adj)	[sa'lʲaðo]
cold (adj)	**frío** (adj)	['frio]
hot (adj)	**caliente** (adj)	[ka'ljente]
bitter (adj)	**amargo** (adj)	[a'marɣo]
tasty (adj)	**sabroso** (adj)	[sa'βroso]
to cook in boiling water	**cocer** (vt) **en agua**	[ko'θer en 'aɣua]
to cook (dinner)	**preparar** (vt)	[prepa'rar]
to fry (vt)	**freír** (vt)	[fre'ir]
to heat up (food)	**calentar** (vt)	[kalen'tar]
to salt (vt)	**salar** (vt)	[sa'lʲar]
to pepper (vt)	**poner pimienta**	[po'ner pi'mjenta]
to grate (vt)	**rallar** (vt)	[ra'jar]
peel (n)	**piel** (f)	[pjelʲ]
to peel (vt)	**pelar** (vt)	[pe'lʲar]

52. Food

meat	**carne** (f)	['karne]
chicken	**gallina** (f)	[ga'jina]
Rock Cornish hen (poussin)	**pollo** (m)	['pojo]
duck	**pato** (m)	['pato]
goose	**ganso** (m)	['ganso]
game	**caza** (f) **menor**	['kaθa me'nor]
turkey	**pava** (f)	['paβa]
pork	**carne** (f) **de cerdo**	['karne de 'θerðo]
veal	**carne** (f) **de ternera**	['karne de ter'nera]
lamb	**carne** (f) **de carnero**	['karne de kar'nero]

beef	**carne** (f) **de vaca**	['karne de 'baka]
rabbit	**conejo** (m)	[ko'neχo]
sausage (bologna, pepperoni, etc.)	**salchichón** (m)	[salʲʧi'ʧon]
vienna sausage (frankfurter)	**salchicha** (f)	[salʲ'ʧiʧa]
bacon	**beicon** (m)	['bejkon]
ham	**jamón** (m)	[χa'mon]
gammon	**jamón** (m) **fresco**	[χa'mon 'fresko]
pâté	**paté** (m)	[pa'te]
liver	**hígado** (m)	['iɣaðo]
hamburger (ground beef)	**carne** (f) **picada**	['karne pi'kaða]
tongue	**lengua** (f)	['lengua]
egg	**huevo** (m)	[u'eβo]
eggs	**huevos** (m pl)	[u'eβos]
egg white	**clara** (f)	['klʲara]
egg yolk	**yema** (f)	['jema]
fish	**pescado** (m)	[pes'kaðo]
seafood	**mariscos** (m pl)	[ma'riskos]
crustaceans	**crustáceos** (m pl)	[krus'taθeos]
caviar	**caviar** (m)	[ka'βjar]
crab	**cangrejo** (m) **de mar**	[kan'greχo de 'mar]
shrimp	**camarón** (m)	[kama'ron]
oyster	**ostra** (f)	['ostra]
spiny lobster	**langosta** (f)	[lʲan'gosta]
octopus	**pulpo** (m)	['pulʲpo]
squid	**calamar** (m)	[kalʲa'mar]
sturgeon	**esturión** (m)	[estu'rjon]
salmon	**salmón** (m)	[salʲ'mon]
halibut	**fletán** (m)	[fle'tan]
cod	**bacalao** (m)	[baka'lʲao]
mackerel	**caballa** (f)	[ka'βaja]
tuna	**atún** (m)	[a'tun]
eel	**anguila** (f)	[an'gilʲa]
trout	**trucha** (f)	['truʧa]
sardine	**sardina** (f)	[sar'ðina]
pike	**lucio** (m)	['lʲuθjo]
herring	**arenque** (m)	[a'reŋke]
bread	**pan** (m)	[pan]
cheese	**queso** (m)	['keso]
sugar	**azúcar** (m)	[a'θukar]
salt	**sal** (f)	[salʲ]
rice	**arroz** (m)	[a'roθ]

pasta (macaroni)	**macarrones** (m pl)	[maka'rones]
noodles	**tallarines** (m pl)	[taja'rines]
butter	**mantequilla** (f)	[mante'kija]
vegetable oil	**aceite** (m) **vegetal**	[a'θejte beχe'talʲ]
sunflower oil	**aceite** (m) **de girasol**	[a'θejte de χira'solʲ]
margarine	**margarina** (f)	[marɣa'rina]
olives	**olivas** (f pl)	[o'liβas]
olive oil	**aceite** (m) **de oliva**	[a'θejte de o'liβa]
milk	**leche** (f)	['leʧe]
condensed milk	**leche** (f) **condensada**	['leʧe konden'saða]
yogurt	**yogur** (m)	[jo'ɣur]
sour cream	**nata** (f) **agria**	['nata 'aɣrja]
cream (of milk)	**nata** (f) **líquida**	['nata 'likiða]
mayonnaise	**mayonesa** (f)	[majo'nesa]
buttercream	**crema** (f) **de mantequilla**	['krema de mante'kija]
cereal grains (wheat, etc.)	**cereal molido grueso**	[θere'alʲ mo'liðo gru'eso]
flour	**harina** (f)	[a'rina]
canned food	**conservas** (f pl)	[kon'serβas]
cornflakes	**copos** (m pl) **de maíz**	['kopos de ma'iθ]
honey	**miel** (f)	[mjelʲ]
jam	**confitura** (f)	[koɱfi'tura]
chewing gum	**chicle** (m)	['ʧikle]

53. Drinks

water	**agua** (f)	['aɣua]
drinking water	**agua** (f) **potable**	['aɣua po'taβle]
mineral water	**agua** (f) **mineral**	['aɣua mine'ralʲ]
still (adj)	**sin gas**	[sin 'gas]
carbonated (adj)	**gaseoso** (adj)	[gase'oso]
sparkling (adj)	**con gas**	[kon 'gas]
ice	**hielo** (m)	['jelo]
with ice	**con hielo**	[kon 'jelo]
non-alcoholic (adj)	**sin alcohol**	[sin alʲko'olʲ]
soft drink	**bebida** (f) **sin alcohol**	[be'βiða sin alʲko'olʲ]
refreshing drink	**refresco** (m)	[re'fresko]
lemonade	**limonada** (f)	[limo'naða]
liquors	**bebidas** (f pl) **alcohólicas**	[be'βiðas alʲko'olikas]
wine	**vino** (m)	['bino]
white wine	**vino** (m) **blanco**	['bino 'blʲaŋko]
red wine	**vino** (m) **tinto**	['bino 'tinto]

liqueur	**licor** (m)	[li'kor]
champagne	**champaña** (f)	[ʧam'panja]
vermouth	**vermú** (m)	[ber'mu]
whiskey	**whisky** (m)	['wiski]
vodka	**vodka** (m)	['boðka]
gin	**ginebra** (f)	[χi'neβra]
cognac	**coñac** (m)	[ko'njak]
rum	**ron** (m)	[ron]
coffee	**café** (m)	[ka'fe]
black coffee	**café** (m) **solo**	[ka'fe 'solo]
coffee with milk	**café** (m) **con leche**	[ka'fe kon 'leʧe]
cappuccino	**capuchino** (m)	[kapu'ʧino]
instant coffee	**café** (m) **soluble**	[ka'fe so'lʲuβle]
milk	**leche** (f)	['leʧe]
cocktail	**cóctel** (m)	['koktelʲ]
milkshake	**batido** (m)	[ba'tiðo]
juice	**zumo** (m), **jugo** (m)	['θumo], ['χuɣo]
tomato juice	**jugo** (m) **de tomate**	['χuɣo de to'mate]
orange juice	**zumo** (m) **de naranja**	['θumo de na'ranχa]
freshly squeezed juice	**zumo** (m) **fresco**	['θumo 'fresko]
beer	**cerveza** (f)	[θer'βeθa]
light beer	**cerveza** (f) **rubia**	[θer'βeθa 'ruβja]
dark beer	**cerveza** (f) **negra**	[θer'βeθa 'neɣra]
tea	**té** (m)	[te]
black tea	**té** (m) **negro**	['te 'neɣro]
green tea	**té** (m) **verde**	['te 'berðe]

54. Vegetables

vegetables	**legumbres** (f pl)	[le'ɣumbres]
greens	**verduras** (f pl)	[ber'ðuras]
tomato	**tomate** (m)	[to'mate]
cucumber	**pepino** (m)	[pe'pino]
carrot	**zanahoria** (f)	[θana'orja]
potato	**patata** (f)	[pa'tata]
onion	**cebolla** (f)	[θe'βoja]
garlic	**ajo** (m)	['aχo]
cabbage	**col** (f)	[kolʲ]
cauliflower	**coliflor** (f)	[koli'flor]
Brussels sprouts	**col** (f) **de Bruselas**	[kolʲ de bru'selʲas]
broccoli	**brócoli** (m)	['brokoli]
beetroot	**remolacha** (f)	[remo'lʲaʧa]

eggplant	**berenjena** (f)	[beren'χena]
zucchini	**calabacín** (m)	[kalʲaβa'θin]
pumpkin	**calabaza** (f)	[kalʲa'βaθa]
turnip	**nabo** (m)	['naβo]
parsley	**perejil** (m)	[pere'χilʲ]
dill	**eneldo** (m)	[e'nelʲðo]
lettuce	**lechuga** (f)	[le'ʧuɣa]
celery	**apio** (m)	['apjo]
asparagus	**espárrago** (m)	[es'paraɣo]
spinach	**espinaca** (f)	[espi'naka]
pea	**guisante** (m)	[gi'sante]
beans	**habas** (f pl)	['aβas]
corn (maize)	**maíz** (m)	[ma'iθ]
kidney bean	**fréjol** (m)	['freχolʲ]
bell pepper	**pimentón** (m)	[pimen'ton]
radish	**rábano** (m)	['raβano]
artichoke	**alcachofa** (f)	[alʲka'ʧofa]

55. Fruits. Nuts

fruit	**fruto** (m)	['fruto]
apple	**manzana** (f)	[man'θana]
pear	**pera** (f)	['pera]
lemon	**limón** (m)	[li'mon]
orange	**naranja** (f)	[na'ranχa]
strawberry (garden ~)	**fresa** (f)	['fresa]
mandarin	**mandarina** (f)	[manda'rina]
plum	**ciruela** (f)	[θiru'elʲa]
peach	**melocotón** (m)	[meloko'ton]
apricot	**albaricoque** (m)	[alʲβari'koke]
raspberry	**frambuesa** (f)	[frambu'esa]
pineapple	**ananás** (m)	[ana'nas]
banana	**banana** (f)	[ba'nana]
watermelon	**sandía** (f)	[san'dia]
grape	**uva** (f)	['uβa]
sour cherry	**guinda** (f)	['ginda]
sweet cherry	**cereza** (f)	[θe'reθa]
melon	**melón** (m)	[me'lon]
grapefruit	**pomelo** (m)	[po'melo]
avocado	**aguacate** (m)	[aɣua'kate]
papaya	**papaya** (m)	[pa'paja]
mango	**mango** (m)	['mango]
pomegranate	**granada** (f)	[gra'naða]
redcurrant	**grosella** (f) **roja**	[gro'seja 'roχa]

blackcurrant	**grosella** (f) **negra**	[gro'seja 'neɣra]
gooseberry	**grosella** (f) **espinosa**	[gro'seja espi'nosa]
bilberry	**arándano** (m)	[a'randano]
blackberry	**zarzamoras** (f pl)	[θarθa'moras]
raisin	**pasas** (f pl)	['pasas]
fig	**higo** (m)	['iɣo]
date	**dátil** (m)	['datilʲ]
peanut	**cacahuete** (m)	[kakau'ete]
almond	**almendra** (f)	[alʲ'mendra]
walnut	**nuez** (f)	[nu'eθ]
hazelnut	**avellana** (f)	[aβe'jana]
coconut	**nuez** (f) **de coco**	[nu'eθ de 'koko]
pistachios	**pistachos** (m pl)	[pis'taʧos]

56. Bread. Candy

bakers' confectionery (pastry)	**pasteles** (m pl)	[pas'teles]
bread	**pan** (m)	[pan]
cookies	**galletas** (f pl)	[ga'jetas]
chocolate (n)	**chocolate** (m)	[ʧoko'lʲate]
chocolate (as adj)	**de chocolate** (adj)	[de ʧoko'lʲate]
candy (wrapped)	**caramelo** (m)	[kara'melo]
cake (e.g., cupcake)	**tarta** (f)	['tarta]
cake (e.g., birthday ~)	**tarta** (f)	['tarta]
pie (e.g., apple ~)	**pastel** (m)	[pas'telʲ]
filling (for cake, pie)	**relleno** (m)	[re'jeno]
jam (whole fruit jam)	**confitura** (f)	[koɱfi'tura]
marmalade	**mermelada** (f)	[merme'lʲaða]
waffles	**gofre** (m)	['gofre]
ice-cream	**helado** (m)	[e'lʲaðo]
pudding	**pudín** (f)	[pu'ðin]

57. Spices

salt	**sal** (f)	[salʲ]
salty (adj)	**salado** (adj)	[sa'lʲaðo]
to salt (vt)	**salar** (vt)	[sa'lʲar]
black pepper	**pimienta** (f) **negra**	[pi'mjenta 'neɣra]
red pepper (milled ~)	**pimienta** (f) **roja**	[pi'mjenta 'roχa]
mustard	**mostaza** (f)	[mos'taθa]
horseradish	**rábano** (m) **picante**	['raβano pi'kante]

condiment	**condimento** (m)	[kondi'mento]
spice	**especia** (f)	[es'peθja]
sauce	**salsa** (f)	['salʲsa]
vinegar	**vinagre** (m)	[bi'naɣre]
anise	**anís** (m)	[a'nis]
basil	**albahaca** (f)	[alʲβa'aka]
cloves	**clavo** (m)	['klʲaβo]
ginger	**jengibre** (m)	[χen'χiβre]
coriander	**cilantro** (m)	[θi'lʲantro]
cinnamon	**canela** (f)	[ka'nelʲa]
sesame	**sésamo** (m)	['sesamo]
bay leaf	**hoja** (f) **de laurel**	['oχa de lʲau'relʲ]
paprika	**páprika** (f)	['paprika]
caraway	**comino** (m)	[ko'mino]
saffron	**azafrán** (m)	[aθa'fran]

PERSONAL INFORMATION. FAMILY

T&P Books Publishing

58. Personal information. Forms

name (first name)	**nombre** (m)	['nombre]
surname (last name)	**apellido** (m)	[ape'jiðo]
date of birth	**fecha** (f) **de nacimiento**	['fetʃa de naθi'mjento]
place of birth	**lugar** (m) **de nacimiento**	[lʲu'ɣar de naθi'mjento]
nationality	**nacionalidad** (f)	[naθjonali'ðað]
place of residence	**domicilio** (m)	[domi'θiljo]
country	**país** (m)	[pa'is]
profession (occupation)	**profesión** (f)	[profe'sjon]
gender, sex	**sexo** (m)	['sekso]
height	**estatura** (f)	[esta'tura]
weight	**peso** (m)	['peso]

59. Family members. Relatives

mother	**madre** (f)	['maðre]
father	**padre** (m)	['paðre]
son	**hijo** (m)	['iχo]
daughter	**hija** (f)	['iχa]
younger daughter	**hija** (f) **menor**	['iχa me'nor]
younger son	**hijo** (m) **menor**	['iχo me'nor]
eldest daughter	**hija** (f) **mayor**	['iχa ma'jor]
eldest son	**hijo** (m) **mayor**	['iχo ma'jor]
brother	**hermano** (m)	[er'mano]
sister	**hermana** (f)	[er'mana]
cousin (masc.)	**primo** (m)	['primo]
cousin (fem.)	**prima** (f)	['prima]
mom, mommy	**mamá** (f)	[ma'ma]
dad, daddy	**papá** (m)	[pa'pa]
parents	**padres** (m pl)	['paðres]
child	**niño** (m), **niña** (f)	['ninjo], ['ninja]
children	**niños** (m pl)	['ninjos]
grandmother	**abuela** (f)	[aβu'elʲa]
grandfather	**abuelo** (m)	[aβu'elo]
grandson	**nieto** (m)	['njeto]
granddaughter	**nieta** (f)	['njeta]
grandchildren	**nietos** (m pl)	['njetos]

uncle	**tío** (m)	['tio]
aunt	**tía** (f)	['tia]
nephew	**sobrino** (m)	[so'βrino]
niece	**sobrina** (f)	[so'βrina]
mother-in-law (wife's mother)	**suegra** (f)	[su'eɣra]
father-in-law (husband's father)	**suegro** (m)	[su'eɣro]
son-in-law (daughter's husband)	**yerno** (m)	['jerno]
stepmother	**madrastra** (f)	[ma'ðrastra]
stepfather	**padrastro** (m)	[pa'ðrastro]
infant	**niño** (m) **de pecho**	['ninjo de 'peʧo]
baby (infant)	**bebé** (m)	[be'βe]
little boy, kid	**chico** (m)	['ʧiko]
wife	**mujer** (f)	[mu'χer]
husband	**marido** (m)	[ma'riðo]
spouse (husband)	**esposo** (m)	[es'poso]
spouse (wife)	**esposa** (f)	[es'posa]
married (masc.)	**casado** (adj)	[ka'saðo]
married (fem.)	**casada** (adj)	[ka'saða]
single (unmarried)	**soltero** (adj)	[solʲ'tero]
bachelor	**soltero** (m)	[solʲ'tero]
divorced (masc.)	**divorciado** (adj)	[diβor'θjaðo]
widow	**viuda** (f)	['bjuða]
widower	**viudo** (m)	['bjuðo]
relative	**pariente** (m)	[pa'rjente]
close relative	**pariente** (m) **cercano**	[pa'rjente θer'kano]
distant relative	**pariente** (m) **lejano**	[pa'rjente le'χano]
relatives	**parientes** (m pl)	[pa'rjentes]
orphan (boy)	**huérfano** (m)	[u'erfano]
orphan (girl)	**huérfana** (f)	[u'erfana]
guardian (of a minor)	**tutor** (m)	[tu'tor]
to adopt (a boy)	**ahijar** (vt)	[ai'χar]
to adopt (a girl)	**ahijar** (vt)	[ai'χar]

60. Friends. Coworkers

friend (masc.)	**amigo** (m)	[a'miɣo]
friend (fem.)	**amiga** (f)	[a'miɣa]
friendship	**amistad** (f)	[amis'tað]
to be friends	**ser amigo**	[ser a'miɣo]
buddy (masc.)	**amigote** (m)	[ami'ɣote]
buddy (fem.)	**amiguete** (f)	[ami'ɣete]

partner	**compañero** (m)	[kompa'njero]
chief (boss)	**jefe** (m)	['χefe]
superior (n)	**superior** (m)	[supe'rjor]
subordinate (n)	**subordinado** (m)	[suβorði'naðo]
colleague	**colega** (m, f)	[ko'leɣa]
acquaintance (person)	**conocido** (m)	[kono'θiðo]
fellow traveler	**compañero** (m) **de viaje**	[kompa'njero de 'bjaχe]
classmate	**condiscípulo** (m)	[kondi'θipulo]
neighbor (masc.)	**vecino** (m)	[be'θino]
neighbor (fem.)	**vecina** (f)	[be'θina]
neighbors	**vecinos** (m pl)	[be'θinos]

HUMAN BODY. MEDICINE

T&P Books Publishing

61. Head

head	**cabeza** (f)	[ka'βeθa]
face	**cara** (f)	['kara]
nose	**nariz** (f)	[na'riθ]
mouth	**boca** (f)	['boka]
eye	**ojo** (m)	['oχo]
eyes	**ojos** (m pl)	['oχos]
pupil	**pupila** (f)	[pu'pilʲa]
eyebrow	**ceja** (f)	['θeχa]
eyelash	**pestaña** (f)	[pes'tanja]
eyelid	**párpado** (m)	['parpaðo]
tongue	**lengua** (f)	['lengua]
tooth	**diente** (m)	['djente]
lips	**labios** (m pl)	['lʲaβjos]
cheekbones	**pómulos** (m pl)	['pomulos]
gum	**encía** (f)	[en'θia]
palate	**paladar** (m)	[palʲa'ðar]
nostrils	**ventanas** (f pl)	[ben'tanas]
chin	**mentón** (m)	[men'ton]
jaw	**mandíbula** (f)	[man'diβulʲa]
cheek	**mejilla** (f)	[me'χija]
forehead	**frente** (f)	['frente]
temple	**sien** (f)	[θjen]
ear	**oreja** (f)	[o'reχa]
back of the head	**nuca** (f)	['nuka]
neck	**cuello** (m)	[ku'ejo]
throat	**garganta** (f)	[gar'ɣanta]
hair	**pelo, cabello** (m)	['pelo], [ka'βejo]
hairstyle	**peinado** (m)	[pej'naðo]
haircut	**corte** (m) **de pelo**	['korte de 'pelo]
wig	**peluca** (f)	[pe'lʲuka]
mustache	**bigote** (m)	[bi'ɣote]
beard	**barba** (f)	['barβa]
to have (a beard, etc.)	**tener** (vt)	[te'ner]
braid	**trenza** (f)	['trenθa]
sideburns	**patillas** (f pl)	[pa'tijas]
red-haired (adj)	**pelirrojo** (adj)	[peli'roχo]
gray (hair)	**gris, canoso** (adj)	[gris], [ka'noso]

bald (adj)	**calvo** (adj)	['kalʲβo]
bald patch	**calva** (f)	['kalʲβa]
ponytail	**cola** (f) **de caballo**	['kolʲa de ka'βajo]
bangs	**flequillo** (m)	[fle'kijo]

62. Human body

hand	**mano** (f)	['mano]
arm	**brazo** (m)	['braθo]
finger	**dedo** (m)	['deðo]
thumb	**dedo** (m) **pulgar**	['deðo pulʲ'ɣar]
little finger	**dedo** (m) **meñique**	['deðo me'njike]
nail	**uña** (f)	['unja]
fist	**puño** (m)	['punjo]
palm	**palma** (f)	['palʲma]
wrist	**muñeca** (f)	[mu'njeka]
forearm	**antebrazo** (m)	[ante·'βraθo]
elbow	**codo** (m)	['koðo]
shoulder	**hombro** (m)	['ombro]
leg	**pierna** (f)	['pjerna]
foot	**planta** (f)	['plʲanta]
knee	**rodilla** (f)	[ro'ðija]
calf (part of leg)	**pantorrilla** (f)	[panto'rija]
hip	**cadera** (f)	[ka'ðera]
heel	**talón** (m)	[ta'lon]
body	**cuerpo** (m)	[ku'erpo]
stomach	**vientre** (m)	['bjentre]
chest	**pecho** (m)	['peʧo]
breast	**seno** (m)	['seno]
flank	**lado** (m), **costado** (m)	['lʲaðo], [kos'taðo]
back	**espalda** (f)	[es'palʲða]
lower back	**zona** (f) **lumbar**	['θona lʲum'bar]
waist	**cintura** (f), **talle** (m)	[θin'tura], ['taje]
navel (belly button)	**ombligo** (m)	[om'bliɣo]
buttocks	**nalgas** (f pl)	['nalʲɣas]
bottom	**trasero** (m)	[tra'sero]
beauty mark	**lunar** (m)	[lʲu'nar]
birthmark (café au lait spot)	**marca** (f) **de nacimiento**	['marka de naθi'mjento]
tattoo	**tatuaje** (m)	[tatu'aχe]
scar	**cicatriz** (f)	[sika'triθ]

63. Diseases

sickness	**enfermedad** (f)	[eɱferme'ðað]
to be sick	**estar enfermo**	[es'tar eɱ'fermo]
health	**salud** (f)	[sa'lʲuð]
runny nose (coryza)	**resfriado** (m)	[resfri'aðo]
tonsillitis	**angina** (f)	[an'χina]
cold (illness)	**resfriado** (m)	[resfri'aðo]
to catch a cold	**resfriarse** (vr)	[resfri'arse]
bronchitis	**bronquitis** (f)	[broŋ'kitis]
pneumonia	**pulmonía** (f)	[pulʲmo'nia]
flu, influenza	**gripe** (f)	['gripe]
nearsighted (adj)	**miope** (adj)	[mi'ope]
farsighted (adj)	**présbita** (adj)	['presβita]
strabismus (crossed eyes)	**estrabismo** (m)	[estra'βismo]
cross-eyed (adj)	**estrábico** (m) (adj)	[es'traβiko]
cataract	**catarata** (f)	[kata'rata]
glaucoma	**glaucoma** (f)	[glʲau'koma]
stroke	**insulto** (m)	[in'sulʲto]
heart attack	**ataque** (m) **cardiaco**	[a'take kar'ðjako]
myocardial infarction	**infarto** (m) **de miocardio**	[iɱ'farto de mio'karðjo]
paralysis	**parálisis** (f)	[pa'ralisis]
to paralyze (vt)	**paralizar** (vt)	[parali'θar]
allergy	**alergia** (f)	[a'lerχja]
asthma	**asma** (f)	['asma]
diabetes	**diabetes** (m)	[dja'βetes]
toothache	**dolor** (m) **de muelas**	[do'lor de mu'elʲas]
caries	**caries** (f)	['karies]
diarrhea	**diarrea** (f)	[dja'rea]
constipation	**estreñimiento** (m)	[estrenji'mjento]
stomach upset	**molestia** (f) **estomacal**	[mo'lestja stoma'kalʲ]
food poisoning	**envenenamiento** (m)	[embenena'mjento]
to get food poisoning	**envenenarse** (vr)	[embene'narse]
arthritis	**artritis** (f)	[ar'tritis]
rickets	**raquitismo** (m)	[raki'tismo]
rheumatism	**reumatismo** (m)	[reuma'tismo]
atherosclerosis	**aterosclerosis** (f)	[ateroskle'rosis]
gastritis	**gastritis** (f)	[gas'tritis]
appendicitis	**apendicitis** (f)	[apendi'θitis]
cholecystitis	**colecistitis** (m)	[koleθis'titis]
ulcer	**úlcera** (f)	['ulʲθera]
measles	**sarampión** (m)	[saram'pjon]

rubella (German measles)	**rubeola** (f)	[ruβe'olʲa]
jaundice	**ictericia** (f)	[ikte'riθja]
hepatitis	**hepatitis** (f)	[epa'titis]
schizophrenia	**esquizofrenia** (f)	[eskiθo'frenja]
rabies (hydrophobia)	**rabia** (f)	['raβja]
neurosis	**neurosis** (f)	[neu'rosis]
concussion	**conmoción** (m) **cerebral**	[konmo'θjon θere'βralʲ]
cancer	**cáncer** (m)	['kanθer]
sclerosis	**esclerosis** (f)	[eskle'rosis]
alcoholism	**alcoholismo** (m)	[alʲkoo'lismo]
alcoholic (n)	**alcohólico** (m)	[alʲko'oliko]
syphilis	**sífilis** (f)	['sifilis]
AIDS	**SIDA** (f)	['siða]
tumor	**tumor** (m)	[tu'mor]
fever	**fiebre** (f)	['fjeβre]
malaria	**malaria** (f)	[ma'lʲarja]
gangrene	**gangrena** (f)	[gan'grena]
seasickness	**mareo** (m)	[ma'reo]
epilepsy	**epilepsia** (f)	[epi'lepsja]
epidemic	**epidemia** (f)	[epi'ðemja]
typhus	**tifus** (m)	['tifus]
tuberculosis	**tuberculosis** (f)	[tuβerku'losis]
cholera	**cólera** (f)	['kolera]
plague (bubonic ~)	**peste** (f)	['peste]

64. Symptoms. Treatments. Part 1

symptom	**síntoma** (m)	['sintoma]
temperature	**temperatura** (f)	[tempera'tura]
high temperature (fever)	**fiebre** (f)	['fjeβre]
pulse	**pulso** (m)	['pulʲso]
dizziness (vertigo)	**mareo** (m)	[ma'reo]
hot (adj)	**caliente** (adj)	[ka'ljente]
shivering	**escalofrío** (m)	[eskalo'frio]
pale (e.g., ~ face)	**pálido** (adj)	['paliðo]
cough	**tos** (f)	[tos]
to cough (vi)	**toser** (vi)	[to'ser]
to sneeze (vi)	**estornudar** (vi)	[estornu'ðar]
faint	**desmayo** (m)	[des'majo]
to faint (vi)	**desmayarse** (vr)	[desma'jarse]
bruise (hématome)	**moradura** (f)	[mora'ðura]
bump (lump)	**chichón** (m)	[ʧi'ʧon]

to bang (bump)	**golpearse** (vr)	[golʲpe'arse]
contusion (bruise)	**magulladura** (f)	[maɣuja'ðura]
to get a bruise	**magullarse** (vr)	[maɣu'jarse]
to limp (vi)	**cojear** (vi)	[koχe'ar]
dislocation	**dislocación** (f)	[disloka'θjon]
to dislocate (vt)	**dislocar** (vt)	[dislo'kar]
fracture	**fractura** (f)	[frak'tura]
to have a fracture	**tener una fractura**	[te'ner 'una frak'tura]
cut (e.g., paper ~)	**corte** (m)	['korte]
to cut oneself	**cortarse** (vr)	[kor'tarse]
bleeding	**hemorragia** (f)	[emo'raχja]
burn (injury)	**quemadura** (f)	[kema'ðura]
to get burned	**quemarse** (vr)	[ke'marse]
to prick (vt)	**pincharse** (vr)	[pin'ʧarse]
to prick oneself	**pincharse** (vr)	[pin'ʧarse]
to injure (vt)	**herir** (vt)	[e'rir]
injury	**herida** (f)	[e'riða]
wound	**lesión** (f)	[le'sjon]
trauma	**trauma** (m)	['trauma]
to be delirious	**delirar** (vi)	[deli'rar]
to stutter (vi)	**tartamudear** (vi)	[tartamuðe'ar]
sunstroke	**insolación** (f)	[insolʲa'θjon]

65. Symptoms. Treatments. Part 2

pain, ache	**dolor** (m)	[do'lor]
splinter (in foot, etc.)	**astilla** (f)	[as'tija]
sweat (perspiration)	**sudor** (m)	[su'ðor]
to sweat (perspire)	**sudar** (vi)	[su'ðar]
vomiting	**vómito** (m)	['bomito]
convulsions	**convulsiones** (f)	[kombulʲ'sjones]
pregnant (adj)	**embarazada** (adj)	[embara'θaða]
to be born	**nacer** (vi)	[na'θer]
delivery, labor	**parto** (m)	['parto]
to deliver (~ a baby)	**dar a luz**	[dar a lʲuθ]
abortion	**aborto** (m)	[a'βorto]
breathing, respiration	**respiración** (f)	[respira'θjon]
in-breath (inhalation)	**inspiración** (f)	[inspira'θjon]
out-breath (exhalation)	**espiración** (f)	[espira'θjon]
to exhale (breathe out)	**espirar** (vi)	[espi'rar]
to inhale (vi)	**inspirar** (vi)	[inspi'rar]
disabled person	**inválido** (m)	[im'baliðo]

cripple	**mutilado** (m)	[muti'lʲaðo]
drug addict	**drogadicto** (m)	[droɣ·a'ðikto]
deaf (adj)	**sordo** (adj)	['sorðo]
mute (adj)	**mudo** (adj)	['muðo]
deaf mute (adj)	**sordomudo** (adj)	[sorðo'muðo]
mad, insane (adj)	**loco** (adj)	['loko]
madman (demented person)	**loco** (m)	['loko]
madwoman	**loca** (f)	['loka]
to go insane	**volverse loco**	[bolʲ'βerse 'loko]
gene	**gen** (m)	[χen]
immunity	**inmunidad** (f)	[inmuni'ðað]
hereditary (adj)	**hereditario** (adj)	[ereði'tarjo]
congenital (adj)	**de nacimiento** (adj)	[de naθi'mjento]
virus	**virus** (m)	['birus]
microbe	**microbio** (m)	[mi'kroβjo]
bacterium	**bacteria** (f)	[bak'terja]
infection	**infección** (f)	[iɱfek'θjon]

66. Symptoms. Treatments. Part 3

hospital	**hospital** (m)	[ospi'talʲ]
patient	**paciente** (m)	[pa'θjente]
diagnosis	**diagnosis** (f)	[dja'ɣnosis]
cure	**cura** (f)	['kura]
medical treatment	**tratamiento** (m)	[trata'mjento]
to get treatment	**curarse** (vr)	[ku'rarse]
to treat (~ a patient)	**tratar** (vt)	[tra'tar]
to nurse (look after)	**cuidar** (vt)	[kui'ðar]
care (nursing ~)	**cuidados** (m pl)	[kui'ðaðos]
operation, surgery	**operación** (f)	[opera'θjon]
to bandage (head, limb)	**vendar** (vt)	[ben'dar]
bandaging	**vendaje** (m)	[ben'daχe]
vaccination	**vacunación** (f)	[bakuna'θjon]
to vaccinate (vt)	**vacunar** (vt)	[baku'nar]
injection, shot	**inyección** (f)	[injek'θjon]
to give an injection	**aplicar una inyección**	[apli'kar 'una injek'θjon]
amputation	**amputación** (f)	[amputa'θjon]
to amputate (vt)	**amputar** (vt)	[ampu'tar]
coma	**coma** (m)	['koma]
to be in a coma	**estar en coma**	[es'tar en 'koma]
intensive care	**revitalización** (f)	[reβitaliθa'θjon]

to recover (~ from flu)	**recuperarse** (vr)	[rekupe'rarse]
condition (patient's ~)	**estado** (m)	[es'taðo]
consciousness	**consciencia** (f)	[kon'θjenθja]
memory (faculty)	**memoria** (f)	[me'morja]
to pull out (tooth)	**extraer** (vt)	[ekstra'er]
filling	**empaste** (m)	[em'paste]
to fill (a tooth)	**empastar** (vt)	[empas'tar]
hypnosis	**hipnosis** (f)	[ip'nosis]
to hypnotize (vt)	**hipnotizar** (vt)	[ipnoti'θar]

67. Medicine. Drugs. Accessories

medicine, drug	**medicamento** (m), **droga** (f)	[meðika'mento], ['droɣa]
remedy	**remedio** (m)	[re'meðjo]
to prescribe (vt)	**prescribir**	[preskri'βir]
prescription	**receta** (f)	[re'θeta]
tablet, pill	**tableta** (f)	[ta'βleta]
ointment	**ungüento** (m)	[ungu'ento]
ampule	**ampolla** (f)	[am'poja]
mixture	**mixtura** (f), **mezcla** (f)	[miks'tura], ['meθklʲa]
syrup	**sirope** (m)	[si'rope]
pill	**píldora** (f)	['pilʲðora]
powder	**polvo** (m)	['polʲβo]
gauze bandage	**venda** (f)	['benda]
cotton wool	**algodón** (m)	[alʲɣo'ðon]
iodine	**yodo** (m)	['joðo]
Band-Aid	**tirita** (f), **curita** (f)	[ti'rita], [ku'rita]
eyedropper	**pipeta** (f)	[pi'peta]
thermometer	**termómetro** (m)	[ter'mometro]
syringe	**jeringa** (f)	[χe'ringa]
wheelchair	**silla** (f) **de ruedas**	['sija de ru'eðas]
crutches	**muletas** (f pl)	[mu'letas]
painkiller	**anestésico** (m)	[anes'tesiko]
laxative	**purgante** (m)	[pur'ɣante]
spirits (ethanol)	**alcohol** (m)	[alʲko'olʲ]
medicinal herbs	**hierba** (f) **medicinal**	['jerβa meðiθi'nalʲ]
herbal (~ tea)	**de hierbas** (adj)	[de 'jerβas]

APARTMENT

T&P Books Publishing

68. Apartment

apartment	**apartamento** (m)	[aparta'mento]
room	**habitación** (f)	[aβita'θjon]
bedroom	**dormitorio** (m)	[dormi'torjo]
dining room	**comedor** (m)	[kome'ðor]
living room	**salón** (m)	[sa'lon]
study (home office)	**despacho** (m)	[des'paʧo]
entry room	**antecámara** (f)	[ante'kamara]
bathroom (room with a bath or shower)	**cuarto** (m) **de baño**	[ku'arto de 'banjo]
half bath	**servicio** (m)	[ser'βiθjo]
ceiling	**techo** (m)	['teʧo]
floor	**suelo** (m)	[su'elo]
corner	**rincón** (m)	[rin'kon]

69. Furniture. Interior

furniture	**muebles** (m pl)	[mu'eβles]
table	**mesa** (f)	['mesa]
chair	**silla** (f)	['sija]
bed	**cama** (f)	['kama]
couch, sofa	**sofá** (m)	[so'fa]
armchair	**sillón** (m)	[si'jon]
bookcase	**librería** (f)	[liβre'ria]
shelf	**estante** (m)	[es'tante]
wardrobe	**armario** (m)	[ar'marjo]
coat rack (wall-mounted ~)	**percha** (f)	['perʧa]
coat stand	**perchero** (m) **de pie**	[per'ʧero de pje]
bureau, dresser	**cómoda** (f)	['komoða]
mirror	**espejo** (m)	[es'peχo]
carpet	**tapiz** (m)	[ta'piθ]
rug, small carpet	**alfombra** (f)	[alʲ'fombra]
fireplace	**chimenea** (f)	[ʧime'nea]
candle	**candela** (f)	[kan'delʲa]
candlestick	**candelero** (m)	[kande'lero]
drapes	**cortinas** (f pl)	[kor'tinas]
wallpaper	**empapelado** (m)	[empape'lʲaðo]

blinds (jalousie)	**estor** (m) **de láminas**	[es'tor de 'lʲaminas]
table lamp	**lámpara** (f) **de mesa**	['lʲampara de 'mesa]
wall lamp (sconce)	**candil** (m)	[kan'dilʲ]
floor lamp	**lámpara** (f) **de pie**	['lʲampara de pje]
chandelier	**lámpara** (f) **de araña**	['lʲampara de a'ranja]
leg (of chair, table)	**pata** (f)	['pata]
armrest	**brazo** (m)	['braθo]
back (backrest)	**espaldar** (m)	[espalʲ'ðar]
drawer	**cajón** (m)	[ka'χon]

70. Bedding

bedclothes	**ropa** (f) **de cama**	['ropa de 'kama]
pillow	**almohada** (f)	[alʲmo'aða]
pillowcase	**funda** (f)	['funda]
duvet, comforter	**manta** (f)	['manta]
sheet	**sábana** (f)	['saβana]
bedspread	**sobrecama** (f)	[soβre'kama]

71. Kitchen

kitchen	**cocina** (f)	[ko'θina]
gas	**gas** (m)	[gas]
gas stove (range)	**cocina** (f) **de gas**	[ko'θina de 'gas]
electric stove	**cocina** (f) **eléctrica**	[ko'θina e'lektrika]
oven	**horno** (m)	['orno]
microwave oven	**horno** (m) **microondas**	['orno mikro·'ondas]
refrigerator	**frigorífico** (m)	[friɣo'rifiko]
freezer	**congelador** (m)	[konχelʲa'ðor]
dishwasher	**lavavajillas** (m)	['lʲaβa·βa'χijas]
meat grinder	**picadora** (f) **de carne**	[pika'ðora de 'karne]
juicer	**exprimidor** (m)	[eksprimi'ðor]
toaster	**tostador** (m)	[tosta'ðor]
mixer	**batidora** (f)	[bati'ðora]
coffee machine	**cafetera** (f)	[kafe'tera]
coffee pot	**cafetera** (f)	[kafe'tera]
coffee grinder	**molinillo** (m) **de café**	[moli'nijo de ka'fe]
kettle	**hervidor** (m) **de agua**	[erβi'ðor de 'aɣua]
teapot	**tetera** (f)	[te'tera]
lid	**tapa** (f)	['tapa]
tea strainer	**colador** (m) **de té**	[kolʲa'ðor de te]
spoon	**cuchara** (f)	[ku'ʧara]
teaspoon	**cucharilla** (f)	[kuʧa'rija]

soup spoon	**cuchara** (f) **de sopa**	[ku'ʧara de 'sopa]
fork	**tenedor** (m)	[tene'ðor]
knife	**cuchillo** (m)	[ku'ʧijo]
tableware (dishes)	**vajilla** (f)	[ba'χija]
plate (dinner ~)	**plato** (m)	['plʲato]
saucer	**platillo** (m)	[plʲa'tijo]
shot glass	**vaso** (m) **de chupito**	['baso de ʧu'pito]
glass (tumbler)	**vaso** (m)	['baso]
cup	**taza** (f)	['taθa]
sugar bowl	**azucarera** (f)	[aθuka'rera]
salt shaker	**salero** (m)	[sa'lero]
pepper shaker	**pimentero** (m)	[pimen'tero]
butter dish	**mantequera** (f)	[mante'kera]
stock pot (soup pot)	**cacerola** (f)	[kaθe'rolʲa]
frying pan (skillet)	**sartén** (f)	[sar'ten]
ladle	**cucharón** (m)	[kuʧa'ron]
colander	**colador** (m)	[kolʲa'ðor]
tray (serving ~)	**bandeja** (f)	[ban'deχa]
bottle	**botella** (f)	[bo'teja]
jar (glass)	**tarro** (m) **de vidrio**	['taro de 'biðrjo]
can	**lata** (f) **de hojalata**	['lʲata de o'χalʲata]
bottle opener	**abrebotellas** (m)	[aβre·βo'tejas]
can opener	**abrelatas** (m)	[aβre·'lʲatas]
corkscrew	**sacacorchos** (m)	[saka'korʧos]
filter	**filtro** (m)	['filʲtro]
to filter (vt)	**filtrar** (vt)	[filʲ'trar]
trash, garbage (food waste, etc.)	**basura** (f)	[ba'sura]
trash can (kitchen ~)	**cubo** (m) **de basura**	['kuβo de ba'sura]

72. Bathroom

bathroom	**cuarto** (m) **de baño**	[ku'arto de 'banjo]
water	**agua** (f)	['aɣua]
faucet	**grifo** (m)	['grifo]
hot water	**agua** (f) **caliente**	['aɣua ka'ljente]
cold water	**agua** (f) **fría**	['aɣua 'fria]
toothpaste	**pasta** (f) **de dientes**	['pasta de 'djentes]
to brush one's teeth	**limpiarse los dientes**	[lim'pjarse los 'djentes]
to shave (vi)	**afeitarse** (vr)	[afej'tarse]
shaving foam	**espuma** (f) **de afeitar**	[es'puma de afej'tar]

razor	**maquinilla** (f) **de afeitar**	[maki'nija de afej'tar]
to wash (one's hands, etc.)	**lavar** (vt)	[lʲa'βar]
to take a bath	**darse un baño**	['darse un 'banjo]
shower	**ducha** (f)	['duʧa]
to take a shower	**darse una ducha**	['darse 'una 'duʧa]
bathtub	**baño** (m)	['banjo]
toilet (toilet bowl)	**inodoro** (m)	[ino'ðoro]
sink (washbasin)	**lavabo** (m)	[lʲa'βaβo]
soap	**jabón** (m)	[χa'βon]
soap dish	**jabonera** (f)	[χaβo'nera]
sponge	**esponja** (f)	[es'ponχa]
shampoo	**champú** (m)	[ʧam'pu]
towel	**toalla** (f)	[to'aja]
bathrobe	**bata** (f) **de baño**	['bata de 'banjo]
laundry (process)	**colada** (f), **lavado** (m)	[ko'lʲaða], [lʲa'βaðo]
washing machine	**lavadora** (f)	[lʲaβa'ðora]
to do the laundry	**lavar la ropa**	[lʲa'βar lʲa 'ropa]
laundry detergent	**detergente** (m) **en polvo**	[deter'χente en 'polʲβo]

73. Household appliances

TV set	**televisor** (m)	[teleβi'sor]
tape recorder	**magnetófono** (m)	[maɣne'tofono]
VCR (video recorder)	**vídeo** (m)	['biðeo]
radio	**radio** (f)	['raðjo]
player (CD, MP3, etc.)	**reproductor** (m)	[reproðuk'tor]
video projector	**proyector** (m) **de vídeo**	[projek'tor de 'biðeo]
home movie theater	**sistema** (m) **home cinema**	[sis'tema 'χoum 'θinema]
DVD player	**reproductor** (m) **de DVD**	reproðuk'tor de deβe'de]
amplifier	**amplificador** (m)	[amplifika'ðor]
video game console	**videoconsola** (f)	[biðeo·kon'solʲa]
video camera	**cámara** (f) **de vídeo**	['kamara de 'biðeo]
camera (photo)	**cámara** (f) **fotográfica**	['kamara foto'ɣrafika]
digital camera	**cámara** (f) **digital**	['kamara diχi'talʲ]
vacuum cleaner	**aspirador** (m), **aspiradora** (f)	[aspira'ðor], [aspira'ðora]
iron (e.g., steam ~)	**plancha** (f)	['plʲanʧa]
ironing board	**tabla** (f) **de planchar**	['taβlʲa de plʲan'ʧar]
telephone	**teléfono** (m)	[te'lefono]
cell phone	**teléfono** (m) **móvil**	[te'lefono 'moβilʲ]
typewriter	**máquina** (f) **de escribir**	['makina de eskri'βir]

sewing machine	**máquina** (f) **de coser**	['makina de ko'ser]
microphone	**micrófono** (m)	[mi'krofono]
headphones	**auriculares** (m pl)	[auriku'ʎares]
remote control (TV)	**mando** (m) **a distancia**	['mando a dis'tanθja]
CD, compact disc	**disco compacto** (m)	['disko kom'pakto]
cassette, tape	**casete** (m)	[ka'sete]
vinyl record	**disco** (m) **de vinilo**	['disko de bi'nilo]

THE EARTH. WEATHER

T&P Books Publishing

74. Outer space

space	**cosmos** (m)	['kosmos]
space (as adj)	**espacial, cósmico** (adj)	[espa'θjalʲ], ['kosmiko]
outer space	**espacio** (m) **cósmico**	[es'paθjo 'kosmiko]
world	**mundo** (m)	['mundo]
universe	**universo** (m)	[uni'βerso]
galaxy	**Galaxia** (f)	[ga'lʲaksja]
star	**estrella** (f)	[es'treja]
constellation	**constelación** (f)	[konstelʲa'θjon]
planet	**planeta** (m)	[plʲa'neta]
satellite	**satélite** (m)	[sa'telite]
meteorite	**meteorito** (m)	[meteo'rito]
comet	**cometa** (f)	[ko'meta]
asteroid	**asteroide** (m)	[aste'roiðe]
orbit	**órbita** (f)	['orβita]
to revolve (~ around the Earth)	**girar** (vi)	[χi'rar]
atmosphere	**atmósfera** (f)	[að'mosfera]
the Sun	**Sol** (m)	[solʲ]
solar system	**Sistema** (m) **Solar**	[sis'tema so'lʲar]
solar eclipse	**eclipse** (m) **de Sol**	[e'klipse de solʲ]
the Earth	**Tierra** (f)	['tjera]
the Moon	**Luna** (f)	['lʲuna]
Mars	**Marte** (m)	['marte]
Venus	**Venus** (f)	['benus]
Jupiter	**Júpiter** (m)	['χupiter]
Saturn	**Saturno** (m)	[sa'turno]
Mercury	**Mercurio** (m)	[mer'kurjo]
Uranus	**Urano** (m)	[u'rano]
Neptune	**Neptuno** (m)	[nep'tuno]
Pluto	**Plutón** (m)	[plʲu'ton]
Milky Way	**la Vía Láctea**	[lʲa 'bia 'lʲaktea]
Great Bear (Ursa Major)	**la Osa Mayor**	[lʲa 'osa ma'jor]
North Star	**la Estrella Polar**	[lʲa es'treja po'lʲar]
Martian	**marciano** (m)	[mar'θjano]
extraterrestrial (n)	**extraterrestre** (m)	[ekstrate'restre]

alien	**planetícola** (m)	[plʲane'tikolʲa]
flying saucer	**platillo** (m) **volante**	[plʲa'tijo bo'lʲante]
spaceship	**nave** (f) **espacial**	['naβe espa'θjalʲ]
space station	**estación** (f) **orbital**	[esta'θjon orβi'talʲ]
blast-off	**despegue** (m)	[des'peɣe]
engine	**motor** (m)	[mo'tor]
nozzle	**tobera** (f)	[to'βera]
fuel	**combustible** (m)	[kombus'tiβle]
cockpit, flight deck	**carlinga** (f)	[kar'linga]
antenna	**antena** (f)	[an'tena]
porthole	**ventana** (f)	[ben'tana]
solar panel	**batería** (f) **solar**	[bate'ria so'lʲar]
spacesuit	**escafandra** (f)	[eska'fandra]
weightlessness	**ingravidez** (f)	[ingraβi'ðeθ]
oxygen	**oxígeno** (m)	[o'ksiχeno]
docking (in space)	**atraque** (m)	[a'trake]
to dock (vi, vt)	**realizar el atraque**	[reali'θar elʲ a'trake]
observatory	**observatorio** (m)	[oβserβa'torjo]
telescope	**telescopio** (m)	[teles'kopjo]
to observe (vt)	**observar** (vt)	[oβser'βar]
to explore (vt)	**explorar** (vt)	[eksplo'rar]

75. The Earth

the Earth	**Tierra** (f)	['tjera]
the globe (the Earth)	**globo** (m) **terrestre**	['gloβo te'restre]
planet	**planeta** (m)	[plʲa'neta]
atmosphere	**atmósfera** (f)	[að'mosfera]
geography	**geografía** (f)	[χeoɣra'fia]
nature	**naturaleza** (f)	[natura'leθa]
globe (table ~)	**globo** (m) **terráqueo**	['gloβo te'rakeo]
map	**mapa** (m)	['mapa]
atlas	**atlas** (m)	['atlʲas]
Europe	**Europa** (f)	[eu'ropa]
Asia	**Asia** (f)	['asja]
Africa	**África** (f)	['afrika]
Australia	**Australia** (f)	[aus'tralja]
America	**América** (f)	[a'merika]
North America	**América** (f) **del Norte**	[a'merika delʲ 'norte]
South America	**América** (f) **del Sur**	[a'merika delʲ 'sur]

Antarctica	**Antártida** (f)	[an'tartiða]
the Arctic	**Ártico** (m)	['artiko]

76. Cardinal directions

north	**norte** (m)	['norte]
to the north	**al norte**	[al^j 'norte]
in the north	**en el norte**	[en el^j 'norte]
northern (adj)	**del norte** (adj)	[del^j 'norte]
south	**sur** (m)	[sur]
to the south	**al sur**	[al^j sur]
in the south	**en el sur**	[en el^j sur]
southern (adj)	**del sur** (adj)	[del^j sur]
west	**oeste** (m)	[o'este]
to the west	**al oeste**	[al^j o'este]
in the west	**en el oeste**	[en el^j o'este]
western (adj)	**del oeste** (adj)	[del^j o'este]
east	**este** (m)	['este]
to the east	**al este**	[al^j 'este]
in the east	**en el este**	[en el^j 'este]
eastern (adj)	**del este** (adj)	[del^j 'este]

77. Sea. Ocean

sea	**mar** (m)	[mar]
ocean	**océano** (m)	[o'θeano]
gulf (bay)	**golfo** (m)	['gol^{j}fo]
straits	**estrecho** (m)	[es'tretʃo]
land (solid ground)	**tierra** (f) **firme**	['tjera 'firme]
continent (mainland)	**continente** (m)	[konti'nente]
island	**isla** (f)	['isl^{j}a]
peninsula	**península** (f)	[pe'ninsul^{j}a]
archipelago	**archipiélago** (m)	[artʃipi'el^{j}aɣo]
bay, cove	**bahía** (f)	[ba'ia]
harbor	**puerto** (m)	[pu'erto]
lagoon	**laguna** (f)	[l^{j}a'ɣuna]
cape	**cabo** (m)	['kaβo]
atoll	**atolón** (m)	[ato'lon]
reef	**arrecife** (m)	[are'θife]
coral	**coral** (m)	[ko'ral^j]
coral reef	**arrecife** (m) **de coral**	[are'θife de ko'ral^j]
deep (adj)	**profundo** (adj)	[pro'fundo]

depth (deep water)	**profundidad** (f)	[profundi'ðað]
abyss	**abismo** (m)	[a'βismo]
trench (e.g., Mariana ~)	**fosa** (f) **oceánica**	['fosa oθe'anika]
current (Ocean ~)	**corriente** (f)	[ko'rjente]
to surround (bathe)	**bañar** (vt)	[ba'njar]
shore	**orilla** (f)	[o'rija]
coast	**costa** (f)	['kosta]
flow (flood tide)	**flujo** (m)	['flʲuχo]
ebb (ebb tide)	**reflujo** (m)	[re'flʲuχo]
shoal	**banco** (m) **de arena**	['baŋko de a'rena]
bottom (~ of the sea)	**fondo** (m)	['fondo]
wave	**ola** (f)	['olʲa]
crest (~ of a wave)	**cresta** (f) **de la ola**	['kresta de lʲa 'olʲa]
spume (sea foam)	**espuma** (f)	[es'puma]
storm (sea storm)	**tempestad** (f)	[tempes'tað]
hurricane	**huracán** (m)	[ura'kan]
tsunami	**tsunami** (m)	[tsu'nami]
calm (dead ~)	**bonanza** (f)	[bo'nanθa]
quiet, calm (adj)	**calmo, tranquilo** (adj)	['kalʲmo], [traŋ'kilo]
pole	**polo** (m)	['polo]
polar (adj)	**polar** (adj)	[po'lʲar]
latitude	**latitud** (f)	[lʲati'tuð]
longitude	**longitud** (f)	[lonχi'tuð]
parallel	**paralelo** (m)	[para'lelo]
equator	**ecuador** (m)	[ekua'ðor]
sky	**cielo** (m)	['θjelo]
horizon	**horizonte** (m)	[ori'θonte]
air	**aire** (m)	['ajre]
lighthouse	**faro** (m)	['faro]
to dive (vi)	**bucear** (vi)	[buθe'ar]
to sink (ab. boat)	**hundirse** (vr)	[un'dirse]
treasures	**tesoros** (m pl)	[te'soros]

78. Seas' and Oceans' names

Atlantic Ocean	**océano** (m) **Atlántico**	[o'θeano at'lʲantiko]
Indian Ocean	**océano** (m) **Índico**	[o'θeano 'indiko]
Pacific Ocean	**océano** (m) **Pacífico**	[o'θeano pa'sifiko]
Arctic Ocean	**océano** (m) **Glacial Ártico**	[o'θeano glʲa'θjalʲ 'artiko]
Black Sea	**mar** (m) **Negro**	[mar 'neɣro]
Red Sea	**mar** (m) **Rojo**	[mar 'roχo]

Yellow Sea	**mar** (m) **Amarillo**	[mar ama'rijo]
White Sea	**mar** (m) **Blanco**	[mar 'blʲaŋko]
Caspian Sea	**mar** (m) **Caspio**	[mar 'kaspjo]
Dead Sea	**mar** (m) **Muerto**	[mar mu'erto]
Mediterranean Sea	**mar** (m) **Mediterráneo**	[mar meðite'raneo]
Aegean Sea	**mar** (m) **Egeo**	[mar e'χeo]
Adriatic Sea	**mar** (m) **Adriático**	[mar aðri'atiko]
Arabian Sea	**mar** (m) **Arábigo**	[mar a'raβiɣo]
Sea of Japan	**mar** (m) **del Japón**	[mar delʲ χa'pon]
Bering Sea	**mar** (m) **de Bering**	[mar de 'beriŋ]
South China Sea	**mar** (m) **de la China Meridional**	[mar de lʲa 'ʃina meriðjo'nalʲ]
Coral Sea	**mar** (m) **del Coral**	[mar delʲ ko'ralʲ]
Tasman Sea	**mar** (m) **de Tasmania**	[mar de tas'manja]
Caribbean Sea	**mar** (m) **Caribe**	[mar kari'βe]
Barents Sea	**mar** (m) **de Barents**	[mar de ba'rents]
Kara Sea	**mar** (m) **de Kara**	[mar de 'kara]
North Sea	**mar** (m) **del Norte**	['mar delʲ 'norte]
Baltic Sea	**mar** (m) **Báltico**	[mar 'baltiko]
Norwegian Sea	**mar** (m) **de Noruega**	[mar de noru'eɣa]

79. Mountains

mountain	**montaña** (f)	[mon'tanja]
mountain range	**cadena** (f) **de montañas**	[ka'ðena de mon'tanjas]
mountain ridge	**cresta** (f) **de montañas**	['kresta de mon'tanjas]
summit, top	**cima** (f)	['θima]
peak	**pico** (m)	['piko]
foot (~ of the mountain)	**pie** (m)	[pje]
slope (mountainside)	**cuesta** (f)	[ku'esta]
volcano	**volcán** (m)	[bolʲ'kan]
active volcano	**volcán** (m) **activo**	[bolʲ'kan ak'tiβo]
dormant volcano	**volcán** (m) **apagado**	[bolʲ'kan apa'ɣaðo]
eruption	**erupción** (f)	[erup'θjon]
crater	**cráter** (m)	['krater]
magma	**magma** (f)	['maɣma]
lava	**lava** (f)	['lʲaβa]
molten (~ lava)	**fundido** (adj)	[fun'diðo]
canyon	**cañón** (m)	[ka'njon]
gorge	**desfiladero** (m)	[desfilʲa'ðero]

crevice	**grieta** (f)	[gri'eta]
abyss (chasm)	**precipicio** (m)	[preθi'piθjo]
pass, col	**puerto** (m)	[pu'erto]
plateau	**meseta** (f)	[me'seta]
cliff	**roca** (f)	['roka]
hill	**colina** (f)	[ko'lina]
glacier	**glaciar** (m)	[glʲa'θjar]
waterfall	**cascada** (f)	[kas'kaða]
geyser	**geiser** (m)	['χejser]
lake	**lago** (m)	['lʲaɣo]
plain	**llanura** (f)	[ja'nura]
landscape	**paisaje** (m)	[paj'saχe]
echo	**eco** (m)	['eko]
alpinist	**alpinista** (m)	[alʲpi'nista]
rock climber	**escalador** (m)	[eskalʲa'ðor]
to conquer (in climbing)	**conquistar** (vt)	[koŋkis'tar]
climb (an easy ~)	**ascensión** (f)	[aθen'sjon]

80. Mountains names

The Alps	**Alpes** (m pl)	['alʲpes]
Mont Blanc	**Montblanc** (m)	[mon'blʲan]
The Pyrenees	**Pirineos** (m pl)	[piri'neos]
The Carpathians	**Cárpatos** (m pl)	['karpatos]
The Ural Mountains	**Urales** (m pl)	[u'rales]
The Caucasus Mountains	**Cáucaso** (m)	['kaukaso]
Mount Elbrus	**Elbrus** (m)	['elʲβrus]
The Altai Mountains	**Altai** (m)	[alʲ'taj]
The Tian Shan	**Tian-Shan** (m)	['tjan 'ʃan]
The Pamir Mountains	**Pamir** (m)	[pa'mir]
The Himalayas	**Himalayos** (m pl)	[ima'lʲajos]
Mount Everest	**Everest** (m)	[eβe'rest]
The Andes	**Andes** (m pl)	['andes]
Mount Kilimanjaro	**Kilimanjaro** (m)	[kiliman'χaro]

81. Rivers

river	**río** (m)	['rio]
spring (natural source)	**manantial** (m)	[manan'tjalʲ]
riverbed (river channel)	**lecho** (m)	['leʧo]
basin (river valley)	**cuenca** (f) **fluvial**	[ku'eŋka flʲu'βjalʲ]

to flow into ...	**desembocar en ...**	[desembo'kar en]
tributary	**afluente** (m)	[aflʲu'ente]
bank (of river)	**orilla** (f), **ribera** (f)	[o'rija], [ri'βera]
current (stream)	**corriente** (f)	[ko'rjente]
downstream (adv)	**río abajo** (adv)	['rio a'βaχo]
upstream (adv)	**río arriba** (adv)	['rio a'riβa]
inundation	**inundación** (f)	[inunda'θjon]
flooding	**riada** (f)	['rjaða]
to overflow (vi)	**desbordarse** (vr)	[desβor'ðarse]
to flood (vt)	**inundar** (vt)	[inun'dar]
shallow (shoal)	**bajo** (m) **arenoso**	['baχo are'noso]
rapids	**rápido** (m)	['rapiðo]
dam	**presa** (f)	['presa]
canal	**canal** (m)	[ka'nalʲ]
reservoir (artificial lake)	**lago** (m) **artificiale**	['laɣo artifi'θjale]
sluice, lock	**esclusa** (f)	[es'klʲusa]
water body (pond, etc.)	**cuerpo** (m) **de agua**	[ku'erpo de 'aɣua]
swamp (marshland)	**pantano** (m)	[pan'tano]
bog, marsh	**ciénaga** (m)	['θjenaɣa]
whirlpool	**remolino** (m)	[remo'lino]
stream (brook)	**arroyo** (m)	[a'rojo]
drinking (ab. water)	**potable** (adj)	[po'taβle]
fresh (~ water)	**dulce** (adj)	['dulʲθe]
ice	**hielo** (m)	['jelo]
to freeze over (ab. river, etc.)	**helarse** (vr)	[e'lʲarse]

82. Rivers' names

Seine	**Sena** (m)	['sena]
Loire	**Loira** (m)	[lu'ara]
Thames	**Támesis** (m)	['tamesis]
Rhine	**Rin** (m)	[rin]
Danube	**Danubio** (m)	[da'nuβjo]
Volga	**Volga** (m)	['bolʲɣa]
Don	**Don** (m)	[don]
Lena	**Lena** (m)	['lena]
Yellow River	**Río** (m) **Amarillo**	['rio ama'rijo]
Yangtze	**Río** (m) **Azul**	['rio a'θulʲ]
Mekong	**Mekong** (m)	[me'koŋ]

Ganges	**Ganges** (m)	['ganges]
Nile River	**Nilo** (m)	['nilo]
Congo River	**Congo** (m)	['kongo]
Okavango River	**Okavango** (m)	[oka'βango]
Zambezi River	**Zambeze** (m)	[sam'beθe]
Limpopo River	**Limpopo** (m)	[limpo'po]

83. Forest

forest, wood	**bosque** (m)	['boske]
forest (as adj)	**de bosque** (adj)	[de 'boske]
thick forest	**espesura** (f)	[espe'sura]
grove	**bosquecillo** (m)	[bokse'θijo]
forest clearing	**claro** (m)	['klʲaro]
thicket	**maleza** (f)	[ma'leθa]
scrubland	**matorral** (m)	[mato'ralʲ]
footpath (troddenpath)	**senda** (f)	['senda]
gully	**barranco** (m)	[ba'raŋko]
tree	**árbol** (m)	['arβolʲ]
leaf	**hoja** (f)	['oχa]
leaves (foliage)	**follaje** (m)	[fo'jaχe]
fall of leaves	**caída** (f) **de hojas**	[ka'iða de 'oχas]
to fall (ab. leaves)	**caer** (vi)	[ka'er]
top (of the tree)	**cima** (f)	['θima]
branch	**rama** (f)	['rama]
bough	**rama** (f)	['rama]
bud (on shrub, tree)	**brote** (m)	['brote]
needle (of pine tree)	**aguja** (f)	[a'ɣuχa]
pine cone	**piña** (f)	['pinja]
hollow (in a tree)	**agujero** (m)	[aɣu'χero]
nest	**nido** (m)	['niðo]
burrow (animal hole)	**madriguera** (f)	[maðri'ɣera]
trunk	**tronco** (m)	['troŋko]
root	**raíz** (f)	[ra'iθ]
bark	**corteza** (f)	[kor'teθa]
moss	**musgo** (m)	['musɣo]
to uproot (remove trees or tree stumps)	**extirpar** (vt)	[estir'par]
to chop down	**talar** (vt)	[ta'lʲar]
to deforest (vt)	**deforestar** (vt)	[defores'tar]
tree stump	**tocón** (m)	[to'kon]

campfire	**hoguera** (f)	[o'gera]
forest fire	**incendio** (m)	[in'θendjo]
to extinguish (vt)	**apagar** (vt)	[apa'ɣar]
forest ranger	**guarda** (m) **forestal**	[gu'arða fores'talʲ]
protection	**protección** (f)	[protek'θjon]
to protect (~ nature)	**proteger** (vt)	[prote'χer]
poacher	**cazador** (m) **furtivo**	[kaθa'ðor fur'tiβo]
steel trap	**cepo** (m)	['θepo]
to gather, to pick (vt)	**recoger** (vt)	[reko'χer]
to lose one's way	**perderse** (vr)	[per'ðerse]

84. Natural resources

natural resources	**recursos** (m pl) **naturales**	[re'kursos natu'rales]
minerals	**minerales** (m pl)	[mine'rales]
deposits	**depósitos** (m pl)	[de'positos]
field (e.g., oilfield)	**yacimiento** (m)	[jaθi'mjento]
to mine (extract)	**extraer** (vt)	[ekstra'er]
mining (extraction)	**extracción** (f)	[ekstrak'θjon]
ore	**mineral** (m)	[mine'ralʲ]
mine (e.g., for coal)	**mina** (f)	['mina]
shaft (mine ~)	**pozo** (m) **de mina**	['poθo de 'mina]
miner	**minero** (m)	[mi'nero]
gas (natural ~)	**gas** (m)	[gas]
gas pipeline	**gasoducto** (m)	[gaso'ðukto]
oil (petroleum)	**petróleo** (m)	[pe'troleo]
oil pipeline	**oleoducto** (m)	[oleo'ðukto]
oil well	**torre** (f) **petrolera**	['tore petro'lera]
derrick (tower)	**torre** (f) **de sondeo**	['tore de son'deo]
tanker	**petrolero** (m)	[petro'lero]
sand	**arena** (f)	[a'rena]
limestone	**caliza** (f)	[ka'liθa]
gravel	**grava** (f)	['graβa]
peat	**turba** (f)	['turβa]
clay	**arcilla** (f)	[ar'θija]
coal	**carbón** (m)	[kar'βon]
iron (ore)	**hierro** (m)	['jero]
gold	**oro** (m)	['oro]
silver	**plata** (f)	['plʲata]
nickel	**níquel** (m)	['nikelʲ]
copper	**cobre** (m)	['koβre]
zinc	**zinc** (m)	[θiŋk]
manganese	**manganeso** (m)	[manga'neso]

mercury	**mercurio** (m)	[mer'kurjo]
lead	**plomo** (m)	['plomo]
mineral	**mineral** (m)	[mine'ralʲ]
crystal	**cristal** (m)	[kris'talʲ]
marble	**mármol** (m)	['marmolʲ]
uranium	**uranio** (m)	[u'ranjo]

85. Weather

weather	**tiempo** (m)	['tjempo]
weather forecast	**previsión** (m) **del tiempo**	[preβi'sjon delʲ 'tjempo]
temperature	**temperatura** (f)	[tempera'tura]
thermometer	**termómetro** (m)	[ter'mometro]
barometer	**barómetro** (m)	[ba'rometro]
humidity	**humedad** (f)	[ume'ðað]
heat (extreme ~)	**bochorno** (m)	[bo'ʧorno]
hot (torrid)	**tórrido** (adj)	['toriðo]
it's hot	**hace mucho calor**	['aθe 'muʧo ka'lor]
it's warm	**hace calor**	['aθe ka'lor]
warm (moderately hot)	**templado** (adj)	[tem'plaðo]
it's cold	**hace frío**	['aθe 'frio]
cold (adj)	**frío** (adj)	['frio]
sun	**sol** (m)	[solʲ]
to shine (vi)	**brillar** (vi)	[bri'jar]
sunny (day)	**soleado** (adj)	[sole'aðo]
to come up (vi)	**elevarse** (vr)	[ele'βarse]
to set (vi)	**ponerse** (vr)	[po'nerse]
cloud	**nube** (f)	['nuβe]
cloudy (adj)	**nuboso** (adj)	[nu'βoso]
rain cloud	**nubarrón** (m)	[nuβa'ron]
somber (gloomy)	**nublado** (adj)	[nu'βlʲaðo]
rain	**lluvia** (f)	['juβja]
it's raining	**está lloviendo**	[es'ta jo'βjendo]
rainy (~ day, weather)	**lluvioso** (adj)	[juβi'oso]
to drizzle (vi)	**lloviznar** (vi)	[joβiθ'nar]
pouring rain	**aguacero** (m)	[aɣua'θero]
downpour	**chaparrón** (m)	[ʧapa'ron]
heavy (e.g., ~ rain)	**fuerte** (adj)	[fu'erte]
puddle	**charco** (m)	['ʧarko]
to get wet (in rain)	**mojarse** (vr)	[mo'χarse]
fog (mist)	**niebla** (f)	['njeβlʲa]
foggy	**nebuloso** (adj)	[neβu'loso]

snow **nieve** (f) ['njeβe]
it's snowing **está nevando** [es'ta ne'βando]

86. Severe weather. Natural disasters

thunderstorm **tormenta** (f) [tor'menta]
lightning (~ strike) **relámpago** (m) [re'lʲampaɣo]
to flash (vi) **relampaguear** (vi) [relʲampaɣe'ar]

thunder **trueno** (m) [tru'eno]
to thunder (vi) **tronar** (vi) [tro'nar]
it's thundering **está tronando** [es'ta tro'nando]

hail **granizo** (m) [gra'niθo]
it's hailing **está granizando** [es'ta grani'θando]

to flood (vt) **inundar** (vt) [inun'dar]
flood, inundation **inundación** (f) [inunda'θjon]

earthquake **terremoto** (m) [tere'moto]
tremor, quake **sacudida** (f) [saku'ðiða]
epicenter **epicentro** (m) [epi'θentro]

eruption **erupción** (f) [erup'θjon]
lava **lava** (f) ['lʲaβa]

twister **torbellino** (m) [torβe'jino]
tornado **tornado** (m) [tor'naðo]
typhoon **tifón** (m) [ti'fon]

hurricane **huracán** (m) [ura'kan]
storm **tempestad** (f) [tempes'tað]
tsunami **tsunami** (m) [tsu'nami]

cyclone **ciclón** (m) [θik'lon]
bad weather **mal tiempo** (m) [malʲ 'tjempo]
fire (accident) **incendio** (m) [in'θendjo]
disaster **catástrofe** (f) [ka'tastrofe]
meteorite **meteorito** (m) [meteo'rito]

avalanche **avalancha** (f) [aβa'lʲanʧa]
snowslide **alud** (m) **de nieve** [alʲuð de 'njeβe]
blizzard **ventisca** (f) [ben'tiska]
snowstorm **nevasca** (f) [ne'βaska]

FAUNA

T&P Books Publishing

87. Mammals. Predators

predator	**carnívoro** (m)	[kar'niβoro]
tiger	**tigre** (m)	['tiɣre]
lion	**león** (m)	[le'on]
wolf	**lobo** (m)	['loβo]
fox	**zorro** (m)	['θoro]
jaguar	**jaguar** (m)	[χaɣu'ar]
leopard	**leopardo** (m)	[leo'parðo]
cheetah	**guepardo** (m)	[ge'parðo]
black panther	**pantera** (f)	[pan'tera]
puma	**puma** (f)	['puma]
snow leopard	**leopardo** (m) **de las nieves**	[leo'parðo de lʲas 'njeβes]
lynx	**lince** (m)	['linθe]
coyote	**coyote** (m)	[ko'jote]
jackal	**chacal** (m)	[ʧa'kalʲ]
hyena	**hiena** (f)	['jena]

88. Wild animals

animal	**animal** (m)	[ani'malʲ]
beast (animal)	**bestia** (f)	['bestja]
squirrel	**ardilla** (f)	[ar'ðija]
hedgehog	**erizo** (m)	[e'riθo]
hare	**liebre** (f)	['ljeβre]
rabbit	**conejo** (m)	[ko'neχo]
badger	**tejón** (m)	[te'χon]
raccoon	**mapache** (m)	[ma'paʧe]
hamster	**hámster** (m)	['amster]
marmot	**marmota** (f)	[mar'mota]
mole	**topo** (m)	['topo]
mouse	**ratón** (m)	[ra'ton]
rat	**rata** (f)	['rata]
bat	**murciélago** (m)	[mur'θjelʲaɣo]
ermine	**armiño** (m)	[ar'minjo]
sable	**cebellina** (f)	[θeβe'jina]

marten	**marta** (f)	['marta]
weasel	**comadreja** (f)	[koma'ðreχa]
mink	**visón** (m)	[bi'son]
beaver	**castor** (m)	[kas'tor]
otter	**nutria** (f)	['nutrja]
horse	**caballo** (m)	[ka'βajo]
moose	**alce** (m)	['alʲθe]
deer	**ciervo** (m)	['θjerβo]
camel	**camello** (m)	[ka'mejo]
bison	**bisonte** (m)	[bi'sonte]
wisent	**uro** (m)	['uro]
buffalo	**búfalo** (m)	['bufalo]
zebra	**cebra** (f)	['θeβra]
antelope	**antílope** (m)	[an'tilope]
roe deer	**corzo** (m)	['korθo]
fallow deer	**gamo** (m)	['gamo]
chamois	**gamuza** (f)	[ga'muθa]
wild boar	**jabalí** (m)	[χaβa'li]
whale	**ballena** (f)	[ba'jena]
seal	**foca** (f)	['foka]
walrus	**morsa** (f)	['morsa]
fur seal	**oso** (m) **marino**	['oso ma'rino]
dolphin	**delfín** (m)	[delʲ'fin]
bear	**oso** (m)	['oso]
polar bear	**oso** (m) **blanco**	['oso 'blʲaŋko]
panda	**panda** (f)	['panda]
monkey	**mono** (m)	['mono]
chimpanzee	**chimpancé** (m)	[ʧimpan'se]
orangutan	**orangután** (m)	[orangu'tan]
gorilla	**gorila** (m)	[go'rilja]
macaque	**macaco** (m)	[ma'kako]
gibbon	**gibón** (m)	[χi'βon]
elephant	**elefante** (m)	[ele'fante]
rhinoceros	**rinoceronte** (m)	[rinoθe'ronte]
giraffe	**jirafa** (f)	[χi'rafa]
hippopotamus	**hipopótamo** (m)	[ipo'potamo]
kangaroo	**canguro** (m)	[kan'guro]
koala (bear)	**koala** (f)	[ko'alʲa]
mongoose	**mangosta** (f)	[man'gosta]
chinchilla	**chinchilla** (f)	[ʧin'ʧija]
skunk	**mofeta** (f)	[mo'feta]
porcupine	**espín** (m)	[es'pin]

89. Domestic animals

tomcat	**gato** (m)	['gato]
dog	**perro** (m)	['pero]
horse	**caballo** (m)	[ka'βajo]
stallion (male horse)	**garañón** (m)	[gara'njon]
mare	**yegua** (f)	['jeɣua]
cow	**vaca** (f)	['baka]
bull	**toro** (m)	['toro]
ox	**buey** (m)	[bu'ej]
sheep (ewe)	**oveja** (f)	[o'βeχa]
ram	**carnero** (m)	[kar'nero]
goat	**cabra** (f)	['kaβra]
billy goat, he-goat	**cabrón** (m)	[ka'βron]
donkey	**asno** (m)	['asno]
mule	**mulo** (m)	['mulo]
pig, hog	**cerdo** (m)	['θerðo]
piglet	**cerdito** (m)	[θer'ðito]
rabbit	**conejo** (m)	[ko'neχo]
hen (chicken)	**gallina** (f)	[ga'jina]
rooster	**gallo** (m)	['gajo]
duck	**pato** (m)	['pato]
drake	**ánade** (m)	['anaðe]
goose	**ganso** (m)	['ganso]
tom turkey, gobbler	**pavo** (m)	['paβo]
turkey (hen)	**pava** (f)	['paβa]
domestic animals	**animales** (m pl) **domésticos**	[ani'males do'mestikos]
tame (e.g., ~ hamster)	**domesticado** (adj)	[domesti'kaðo]
to tame (vt)	**domesticar** (vt)	[domesti'kar]
to breed (vt)	**criar** (vt)	[kri'ar]
farm	**granja** (f)	['granχa]
poultry	**aves** (f pl) **de corral**	['aβes de ko'ralʲ]
cattle	**ganado** (m)	[ga'njaðo]
herd (cattle)	**rebaño** (m)	[re'βanjo]
stable	**caballeriza** (f)	[kaβaje'riθa]
pigpen	**porqueriza** (f)	[porke'riθa]
cowshed	**vaquería** (f)	[bake'ria]
rabbit hutch	**conejal** (m)	[kone'χalʲ]
hen house	**gallinero** (m)	[gaji'nero]

90. Birds

bird	**pájaro** (m)	['paχaro]
pigeon	**paloma** (f)	[pa'loma]
sparrow	**gorrión** (m)	[gori'jon]
tit (great tit)	**paro** (m)	['paro]
magpie	**cotorra** (f)	[ko'tora]
raven	**cuervo** (m)	[ku'erβo]
crow	**corneja** (f)	[kor'neχa]
jackdaw	**chova** (f)	['ʧoβa]
rook	**grajo** (m)	['graχo]
duck	**pato** (m)	['pato]
goose	**ganso** (m)	['ganso]
pheasant	**faisán** (m)	[faj'san]
eagle	**águila** (f)	['aɣilʲa]
hawk	**azor** (m)	[a'θor]
falcon	**halcón** (m)	[alʲ'kon]
vulture	**buitre** (m)	[bu'itre]
condor (Andean ~)	**cóndor** (m)	['kondor]
swan	**cisne** (m)	['θisne]
crane	**grulla** (f)	['gruja]
stork	**cigüeña** (f)	[θiɣu'enja]
parrot	**loro** (m), **papagayo** (m)	['loro], [papa'ɣajo]
hummingbird	**colibrí** (m)	[koli'βri]
peacock	**pavo** (m) **real**	['paβo re'alʲ]
ostrich	**avestruz** (m)	[aβes'truθ]
heron	**garza** (f)	['garθa]
flamingo	**flamenco** (m)	[flʲa'meŋko]
pelican	**pelícano** (m)	[pe'likano]
nightingale	**ruiseñor** (m)	[ruise'njor]
swallow	**golondrina** (f)	[golon'drina]
thrush	**tordo** (m)	['torðo]
song thrush	**zorzal** (m)	[θor'θalʲ]
blackbird	**mirlo** (m)	['mirlo]
swift	**vencejo** (m)	[ben'θeχo]
lark	**alondra** (f)	[a'londra]
quail	**codorniz** (f)	[ko'ðorniθ]
woodpecker	**pico** (m)	['piko]
cuckoo	**cuco** (m)	['kuko]
owl	**lechuza** (f)	[le'ʧuθa]
eagle owl	**búho** (m)	['buo]

wood grouse	**urogallo** (m)	[uro'ɣajo]
black grouse	**gallo lira** (m)	['gajo 'lira]
partridge	**perdiz** (f)	[per'ðiθ]
starling	**estornino** (m)	[estor'nino]
canary	**canario** (m)	[ka'narjo]
hazel grouse	**ortega** (f)	[or'teɣa]
chaffinch	**pinzón** (m)	[pin'θon]
bullfinch	**camachuelo** (m)	[kamatʃu'elo]
seagull	**gaviota** (f)	[ga'βjota]
albatross	**albatros** (m)	[alʲ'βatros]
penguin	**pingüino** (m)	[pingu'ino]

91. Fish. Marine animals

bream	**brema** (f)	['brema]
carp	**carpa** (f)	['karpa]
perch	**perca** (f)	['perka]
catfish	**siluro** (m)	[si'lʲuro]
pike	**lucio** (m)	['lʲuθjo]
salmon	**salmón** (m)	[salʲ'mon]
sturgeon	**esturión** (m)	[estu'rjon]
herring	**arenque** (m)	[a'reŋke]
Atlantic salmon	**salmón** (m) **del Atlántico**	[salʲ'mon delʲ at'lʲantiko]
mackerel	**caballa** (f)	[ka'βaja]
flatfish	**lenguado** (m)	[lengu'aðo]
zander, pike perch	**lucioperca** (m)	[lʲuθjo'perka]
cod	**bacalao** (m)	[baka'lʲao]
tuna	**atún** (m)	[a'tun]
trout	**trucha** (f)	['trutʃa]
eel	**anguila** (f)	[an'gilʲa]
electric ray	**tembladera** (f)	[temblʲa'ðera]
moray eel	**morena** (f)	[mo'rena]
piranha	**piraña** (f)	[pi'ranja]
shark	**tiburón** (m)	[tiβu'ron]
dolphin	**delfín** (m)	[delʲ'fin]
whale	**ballena** (f)	[ba'jena]
crab	**centolla** (f)	[θen'toja]
jellyfish	**medusa** (f)	[me'ðusa]
octopus	**pulpo** (m)	['pulʲpo]
starfish	**estrella** (f) **de mar**	[es'treja de mar]
sea urchin	**erizo** (m) **de mar**	[e'riθo de mar]

seahorse	**caballito** (m) **de mar**	[kaβa'jito de mar]
oyster	**ostra** (f)	['ostra]
shrimp	**camarón** (m)	[kama'ron]
lobster	**bogavante** (m)	[boɣa'βante]
spiny lobster	**langosta** (f)	[lʲan'gosta]

92. Amphibians. Reptiles

snake	**serpiente** (f)	[ser'pjente]
venomous (snake)	**venenoso** (adj)	[bene'noso]
viper	**víbora** (f)	['biβora]
cobra	**cobra** (f)	['koβra]
python	**pitón** (m)	[pi'ton]
boa	**boa** (f)	['boa]
grass snake	**culebra** (f)	[ku'leβra]
rattle snake	**serpiente** (m) **de cascabel**	[ser'pjente de kaska'βelʲ]
anaconda	**anaconda** (f)	[ana'konda]
lizard	**lagarto** (f)	[lʲa'ɣarto]
iguana	**iguana** (f)	[iɣu'ana]
monitor lizard	**varano** (m)	[ba'rano]
salamander	**salamandra** (f)	[salʲa'mandra]
chameleon	**camaleón** (m)	[kamale'on]
scorpion	**escorpión** (m)	[eskorpi'on]
turtle	**tortuga** (f)	[tor'tuɣa]
frog	**rana** (f)	['rana]
toad	**sapo** (m)	['sapo]
crocodile	**cocodrilo** (m)	[koko'ðrilo]

93. Insects

insect, bug	**insecto** (m)	[in'sekto]
butterfly	**mariposa** (f)	[mari'posa]
ant	**hormiga** (f)	[or'miɣa]
fly	**mosca** (f)	['moska]
mosquito	**mosquito** (m)	[mos'kito]
beetle	**escarabajo** (m)	[eskara'βaχo]
wasp	**avispa** (f)	[a'βispa]
bee	**abeja** (f)	[a'βeχa]
bumblebee	**abejorro** (m)	[aβe'χoro]
gadfly (botfly)	**moscardón** (m)	[moskar'ðon]
spider	**araña** (f)	[a'ranja]
spiderweb	**telaraña** (f)	[telʲa'ranja]

dragonfly	**libélula** (f)	[li'βelʲulʲa]
grasshopper	**saltamontes** (m)	[salʲta'montes]
moth (night butterfly)	**mariposa** (f) **nocturna**	[mari'posa nok'turna]
cockroach	**cucaracha** (f)	[kuka'ratʃa]
tick	**garrapata** (f)	[gara'pata]
flea	**pulga** (f)	['pulʲɣa]
midge	**mosca** (f) **negra**	['moska 'neɣra]
locust	**langosta** (f)	[lʲan'gosta]
snail	**caracol** (m)	[kara'kolʲ]
cricket	**grillo** (m)	['grijo]
lightning bug	**luciérnaga** (f)	[lʲu'θjernaɣa]
ladybug	**mariquita** (f)	[mari'kita]
leech	**sanguijuela** (f)	[sangiχu'elʲa]
caterpillar	**oruga** (f)	[o'ruɣa]
earthworm	**gusano** (m)	[gu'sano]
larva	**larva** (f)	['lʲarβa]

FLORA

T&P Books Publishing

94. Trees

tree	**árbol** (m)	['arβol^{j}]
deciduous (adj)	**foliáceo** (adj)	[foli'aθeo]
coniferous (adj)	**conífero** (adj)	[ko'nifero]
evergreen (adj)	**de hoja perenne**	[de 'oχa pe'renne]
apple tree	**manzano** (m)	[man'θano]
pear tree	**peral** (m)	[pe'ral^{j}]
sweet cherry tree	**cerezo** (m)	[θe'reθo]
sour cherry tree	**guindo** (m)	['gindo]
plum tree	**ciruelo** (m)	[θiru'elo]
birch	**abedul** (m)	[aβe'ðul^{j}]
oak	**roble** (m)	['roβle]
linden tree	**tilo** (m)	['tilo]
aspen	**pobo** (m)	['poβo]
maple	**arce** (m)	['arθe]
spruce	**picea** (m)	[pi'θea]
pine	**pino** (m)	['pino]
larch	**alerce** (m)	[a'lerθe]
fir tree	**abeto** (m)	[a'βeto]
cedar	**cedro** (m)	['θeðro]
poplar	**álamo** (m)	['al^{j}amo]
rowan	**serbal** (m)	[ser'βal^{j}]
willow	**sauce** (m)	['sauθe]
alder	**aliso** (m)	[a'liso]
beech	**haya** (f)	['aja]
elm	**olmo** (m)	['ol^{j}mo]
ash (tree)	**fresno** (m)	['fresno]
chestnut	**castaño** (m)	[kas'tanjo]
magnolia	**magnolia** (f)	[maɣ'nolja]
palm tree	**palmera** (f)	[pal^{j}'mera]
cypress	**ciprés** (m)	[θi'pres]
mangrove	**mangle** (m)	['mangl]
baobab	**baobab** (m)	[bao'βaβ]
eucalyptus	**eucalipto** (m)	[euka'lipto]
sequoia	**secoya** (f)	[se'koja]

95. Shrubs

bush	**mata** (f)	['mata]
shrub	**arbusto** (m)	[ar'βusto]
grapevine	**vid** (f)	[bið]
vineyard	**viñedo** (m)	[bi'njeðo]
raspberry bush	**frambueso** (m)	[frambu'eso]
redcurrant bush	**grosellero** (f) **rojo**	[grose'jero 'roχo]
gooseberry bush	**grosellero** (m) **espinoso**	[grose'jero espi'noso]
acacia	**acacia** (f)	[a'kaθja]
barberry	**berberís** (m)	[berβe'ris]
jasmine	**jazmín** (m)	[χaθ'min]
juniper	**enebro** (m)	[e'neβro]
rosebush	**rosal** (m)	[ro'salʲ]
dog rose	**escaramujo** (m)	[eskara'muχo]

96. Fruits. Berries

apple	**manzana** (f)	[man'θana]
pear	**pera** (f)	['pera]
plum	**ciruela** (f)	[θiru'elʲa]
strawberry (garden ~)	**fresa** (f)	['fresa]
sour cherry	**guinda** (f)	['ginda]
sweet cherry	**cereza** (f)	[θe'reθa]
grape	**uva** (f)	['uβa]
raspberry	**frambuesa** (f)	[frambu'esa]
blackcurrant	**grosella** (f) **negra**	[gro'seja 'neɣra]
redcurrant	**grosella** (f) **roja**	[gro'seja 'roχa]
gooseberry	**grosella** (f) **espinosa**	[gro'seja espi'nosa]
cranberry	**arándano** (m) **agrio**	[a'randano 'aɣrjo]
orange	**naranja** (f)	[na'ranχa]
mandarin	**mandarina** (f)	[manda'rina]
pineapple	**ananás** (m)	[ana'nas]
banana	**banana** (f)	[ba'nana]
date	**dátil** (m)	['datilʲ]
lemon	**limón** (m)	[li'mon]
apricot	**albaricoque** (m)	[alʲβari'koke]
peach	**melocotón** (m)	[meloko'ton]
kiwi	**kiwi** (m)	['kiwi]
grapefruit	**pomelo** (m)	[po'melo]
berry	**baya** (f)	['baja]

berries	**bayas** (f pl)	['bajas]
cowberry	**arándano** (m) **rojo**	[a'randano 'roχo]
wild strawberry	**fresa** (f) **silvestre**	['fresa silʲ'βestre]
bilberry	**arándano** (m)	[a'randano]

97. Flowers. Plants

flower	**flor** (f)	[flor]
bouquet (of flowers)	**ramo** (m) **de flores**	['ramo de 'flores]
rose (flower)	**rosa** (f)	['rosa]
tulip	**tulipán** (m)	[tuli'pan]
carnation	**clavel** (m)	[klʲa'βelʲ]
gladiolus	**gladiolo** (m)	[glʲa'ðjolo]
cornflower	**aciano** (m)	[a'θjano]
harebell	**campanilla** (f)	[kampa'nija]
dandelion	**diente** (m) **de león**	['djente de le'on]
camomile	**manzanilla** (f)	[manθa'nija]
aloe	**áloe** (m)	['aloe]
cactus	**cacto** (m)	['kakto]
rubber plant, ficus	**ficus** (m)	['fikus]
lily	**azucena** (f)	[aθu'sena]
geranium	**geranio** (m)	[χe'ranjo]
hyacinth	**jacinto** (m)	[χa'θinto]
mimosa	**mimosa** (f)	[mi'mosa]
narcissus	**narciso** (m)	[nar'θiso]
nasturtium	**capuchina** (f)	[kapu'ʧina]
orchid	**orquídea** (f)	[or'kiðea]
peony	**peonía** (f)	[peo'nia]
violet	**violeta** (f)	[bio'leta]
pansy	**trinitaria** (f)	[trini'tarja]
forget-me-not	**nomeolvides** (f)	[nomeolʲ'βiðes]
daisy	**margarita** (f)	[marɣa'rita]
poppy	**amapola** (f)	[ama'polʲa]
hemp	**cáñamo** (m)	['kanjamo]
mint	**menta** (f)	['menta]
lily of the valley	**muguete** (m)	[mu'ɣete]
snowdrop	**campanilla** (f) **de las nieves**	[kampa'nija de lʲas 'njeβes]
nettle	**ortiga** (f)	[or'tiɣa]
sorrel	**acedera** (f)	[aθe'ðera]

water lily	**nenúfar** (m)	[ne'nufar]
fern	**helecho** (m)	[e'letʃo]
lichen	**liquen** (m)	['liken]
greenhouse (tropical ~)	**invernadero** (m)	[imberna'ðero]
lawn	**césped** (m)	['θespeð]
flowerbed	**macizo** (m) **de flores**	[ma'θiθo de 'flores]
plant	**planta** (f)	['plʲanta]
grass	**hierba** (f)	['jerβa]
blade of grass	**hoja** (f) **de hierba**	['oχa de 'jerβa]
leaf	**hoja** (f)	['oχa]
petal	**pétalo** (m)	['petalo]
stem	**tallo** (m)	['tajo]
tuber	**tubérculo** (m)	[tu'βerkulo]
young plant (shoot)	**retoño** (m)	[re'tonjo]
thorn	**espina** (f)	[es'pina]
to blossom (vi)	**florecer** (vi)	[flore'θer]
to fade, to wither	**marchitarse** (vr)	[martʃi'tarse]
smell (odor)	**olor** (m)	[o'lor]
to cut (flowers)	**cortar** (vt)	[kor'tar]
to pick (a flower)	**coger** (vt)	[ko'χer]

98. Cereals, grains

grain	**grano** (m)	['grano]
cereal crops	**cereales** (m pl)	[θere'ales]
ear (of barley, etc.)	**espiga** (f)	[es'piɣa]
wheat	**trigo** (m)	['triɣo]
rye	**centeno** (m)	[θen'teno]
oats	**avena** (f)	[a'βena]
millet	**mijo** (m)	['miχo]
barley	**cebada** (f)	[θe'βaða]
corn	**maíz** (m)	[ma'iθ]
rice	**arroz** (m)	[a'roθ]
buckwheat	**alforfón** (m)	[alʲfor'fon]
pea plant	**guisante** (m)	[gi'sante]
kidney bean	**fréjol** (m)	['freχolʲ]
soy	**soya** (f)	['soja]
lentil	**lenteja** (f)	[len'teχa]
beans (pulse crops)	**habas** (f pl)	['aβas]

COUNTRIES OF THE WORLD

T&P Books Publishing

99. Countries. Part 1

Afghanistan — **Afganistán** (m) [afɣanis'tan]
Albania — **Albania** (f) [alʲ'βanja]
Argentina — **Argentina** (f) [arχen'tina]
Armenia — **Armenia** (f) [ar'menja]
Australia — **Australia** (f) [aus'tralja]
Austria — **Austria** (f) ['austrja]
Azerbaijan — **Azerbaidzhán** (m) [aθerβaj'ʤan]

The Bahamas — **Islas** (f pl) **Bahamas** ['islʲas ba'amas]
Bangladesh — **Bangladesh** (m) [banglʲa'ðeʃ]
Belarus — **Bielorrusia** (f) [bjelo'rusja]
Belgium — **Bélgica** (f) ['belʲχika]
Bolivia — **Bolivia** (f) [bo'liβja]
Bosnia and Herzegovina — **Bosnia y Herzegovina** ['bosnia i erθeχo'βina]
Brazil — **Brasil** (f) [bra'silʲ]
Bulgaria — **Bulgaria** (f) [bul'ɣarja]

Cambodia — **Camboya** (f) [kam'boja]
Canada — **Canadá** (f) [kana'ða]
Chile — **Chile** (m) ['ʧile]
China — **China** (f) ['ʧina]
Colombia — **Colombia** (f) [ko'lombja]
Croatia — **Croacia** (f) [kro'aθja]
Cuba — **Cuba** (f) ['kuβa]
Cyprus — **Chipre** (m) ['ʧipre]
Czech Republic — **Chequia** (f) ['ʧekja]

Denmark — **Dinamarca** (f) [dina'marka]
Dominican Republic — **República** (f) **Dominicana** [re'puβlika domini'kana]
Ecuador — **Ecuador** (m) [ekua'ðor]
Egypt — **Egipto** (m) [e'χipto]
England — **Inglaterra** (f) [inglʲa'tera]
Estonia — **Estonia** (f) [es'tonja]
Finland — **Finlandia** (f) [fin'lʲandja]
France — **Francia** (f) ['franθja]
French Polynesia — **Polinesia** (f) **Francesa** [poli'nesja fran'θesa]

Georgia — **Georgia** (f) [χe'orχja]
Germany — **Alemania** (f) [ale'manja]
Ghana — **Ghana** (f) ['gana]
Great Britain — **Gran Bretaña** (f) [gran bre'tanja]
Greece — **Grecia** (f) ['greθja]
Haiti — **Haití** (m) [ai'ti]
Hungary — **Hungría** (f) [un'gria]

100. Countries. Part 2

Iceland	**Islandia** (f)	[is'lʲandja]
India	**India** (f)	['indja]
Indonesia	**Indonesia** (f)	[indo'nesja]
Iran	**Irán** (m)	[i'ran]
Iraq	**Irak** (m)	[i'rak]
Ireland	**Irlanda** (f)	[ir'lʲanda]
Israel	**Israel** (m)	[isra'elʲ]
Italy	**Italia** (f)	[i'talja]
Jamaica	**Jamaica** (f)	[χa'majka]
Japan	**Japón** (m)	[χa'pon]
Jordan	**Jordania** (f)	[χor'ðanja]
Kazakhstan	**Kazajistán** (m)	[kaθaχi'stan]
Kenya	**Kenia** (f)	['kenja]
Kirghizia	**Kirguizistán** (m)	[kirɣiθi'stan]
Kuwait	**Kuwait** (m)	[ku'wajt]
Laos	**Laos** (m)	[lʲa'os]
Latvia	**Letonia** (f)	[le'tonja]
Lebanon	**Líbano** (m)	['liβano]
Libya	**Libia** (f)	['liβja]
Liechtenstein	**Liechtenstein** (m)	[leχten'stejn]
Lithuania	**Lituania** (f)	[litu'anja]
Luxembourg	**Luxemburgo** (m)	[lʲuksem'burɣo]
Macedonia (Republic of ~)	**Macedonia**	[maθe'ðonja]
Madagascar	**Madagascar** (m)	[maðaɣas'kar]
Malaysia	**Malasia** (f)	[ma'lʲasja]
Malta	**Malta** (f)	['malʲta]
Mexico	**Méjico** (m)	['meχiko]
Moldova, Moldavia	**Moldavia** (f)	[molʲ'ðaβja]
Monaco	**Mónaco** (m)	['monako]
Mongolia	**Mongolia** (f)	[mon'golja]
Montenegro	**Montenegro** (m)	[monte'neɣro]
Morocco	**Marruecos** (m)	[maru'ekos]
Myanmar	**Myanmar** (m)	[mjan'mar]
Namibia	**Namibia** (f)	[na'miβja]
Nepal	**Nepal** (m)	[ne'palʲ]
Netherlands	**Países Bajos** (m pl)	[pa'ises 'baχos]
New Zealand	**Nueva Zelanda** (f)	[nu'eβa θe'lʲanda]
North Korea	**Corea** (f) **del Norte**	[ko'rea delʲ 'norte]
Norway	**Noruega** (f)	[noru'eɣa]

101. Countries. Part 3

Pakistan	**Pakistán** (m)	[pakis'tan]
Palestine	**Palestina** (f)	[pales'tina]

Panama	**Panamá** (f)	[pana'ma]
Paraguay	**Paraguay** (m)	[paraɣu'aj]
Peru	**Perú** (m)	[pe'ru]
Poland	**Polonia** (f)	[po'lonja]
Portugal	**Portugal** (f)	[portu'ɣalʲ]
Romania	**Rumania** (f)	[ru'manja]
Russia	**Rusia** (f)	['rusja]
Saudi Arabia	**Arabia** (f) **Saudita**	[a'raβja sau'ðita]
Scotland	**Escocia** (f)	[es'koθja]
Senegal	**Senegal**	[sene'ɣalʲ]
Serbia	**Serbia** (f)	['serβja]
Slovakia	**Eslovaquia** (f)	[eslo'βakja]
Slovenia	**Eslovenia**	[eslo'βenja]
South Africa	**República** (f) **Sudafricana**	[re'puβlika suð·afri'kana]
South Korea	**Corea** (f) **del Sur**	[ko'rea delʲ sur]
Spain	**España** (f)	[es'panja]
Suriname	**Surinam** (m)	[suri'nam]
Sweden	**Suecia** (f)	[su'eθja]
Switzerland	**Suiza** (f)	[su'isa]
Syria	**Siria** (f)	['sirja]
Taiwan	**Taiwán** (m)	[taj'wan]
Tajikistan	**Tayikistán** (m)	[tajikis'tan]
Tanzania	**Tanzania** (f)	[tan'θanja]
Tasmania	**Tasmania** (f)	[tas'manja]
Thailand	**Tailandia** (f)	[taj'lʲandja]
Tunisia	**Túnez** (m)	['tuneθ]
Turkey	**Turquía** (f)	[tur'kia]
Turkmenistan	**Turkmenia** (f)	[turk'menja]
Ukraine	**Ucrania** (f)	[u'kranja]
United Arab Emirates	**Emiratos** (m pl) **Árabes Unidos**	[emi'rates 'araβes u'niðos]
United States of America	**Estados Unidos de América** (m pl)	[es'tados u'niðos de a'merika]
Uruguay	**Uruguay** (m)	[uruɣu'aj]
Uzbekistan	**Uzbekistán** (m)	[uθβekis'tan]
Vatican	**Vaticano** (m)	[bati'kano]
Venezuela	**Venezuela** (f)	[beneθu'elʲa]
Vietnam	**Vietnam** (m)	[bjet'nam]
Zanzibar	**Zanzíbar** (m)	[θanθi'βar]

GASTRONOMIC GLOSSARY

This section contains a lot of words and terms associated with food. This dictionary will make it easier for you to understand the menu at a restaurant and choose the right dish

T&P Books Publishing

English-Spanish gastronomic glossary

aftertaste	**regusto** (m)	[re'ɣusto]
almond	**almendra** (f)	[alʲ'mendra]
anise	**anís** (m)	[a'nis]
aperitif	**aperitivo** (m)	[aperi'tiβo]
appetite	**apetito** (m)	[ape'tito]
appetizer	**entremés** (m)	[entre'mes]
apple	**manzana** (f)	[man'θana]
apricot	**albaricoque** (m)	[alʲβari'koke]
artichoke	**alcachofa** (f)	[alʲka'ʧofa]
asparagus	**espárrago** (m)	[es'paraɣo]
Atlantic salmon	**salmón** (m) **del Atlántico**	[salʲ'mon delʲ at'lʲantiko]
avocado	**aguacate** (m)	[aɣua'kate]
bacon	**beicon** (m)	['bejkon]
banana	**banana** (f)	[ba'nana]
barley	**cebada** (f)	[θe'βaða]
bartender	**barman** (m)	['barman]
basil	**albahaca** (f)	[alʲβa'aka]
bay leaf	**hoja** (f) **de laurel**	['oχa de lʲau'relʲ]
beans	**habas** (f pl)	['aβas]
beef	**carne** (f) **de vaca**	['karne de 'baka]
beer	**cerveza** (f)	[θer'βeθa]
beetroot	**remolacha** (f)	[remo'lʲaʧa]
bell pepper	**pimentón** (m)	[pimen'ton]
berries	**bayas** (f pl)	['bajas]
berry	**baya** (f)	['baja]
bilberry	**arándano** (m)	[a'randano]
birch bolete	**boleto** (m) **áspero**	[bo'leto 'aspero]
bitter	**amargo** (adj)	[a'marɣo]
black coffee	**café** (m) **solo**	[ka'fe 'solo]
black pepper	**pimienta** (f) **negra**	[pi'mjenta 'neɣra]
black tea	**té** (m) **negro**	['te 'neɣro]
blackberry	**zarzamoras** (f pl)	[θarθa'moras]
blackcurrant	**grosella** (f) **negra**	[gro'seja 'neɣra]
boiled	**cocido en agua** (adj)	[ko'θiðo en 'aɣua]
bottle opener	**abrebotellas** (m)	[aβre·βo'tejas]
bread	**pan** (m)	[pan]
breakfast	**desayuno** (m)	[desa'juno]
bream	**brema** (f)	['brema]
broccoli	**brócoli** (m)	['brokoli]
Brussels sprouts	**col** (f) **de Bruselas**	[kolʲ de bru'selʲas]
buckwheat	**alforfón** (m)	[alʲfor'fon]
butter	**mantequilla** (f)	[mante'kija]
buttercream	**crema** (f) **de mantequilla**	['krema de mante'kija]
cabbage	**col** (f)	[kolʲ]

cake	**tarta** (f)	['tarta]
cake	**tarta** (f)	['tarta]
calorie	**caloría** (f)	[kalo'ria]
can opener	**abrelatas** (m)	[aβre·'lʲatas]
candy	**caramelo** (m)	[kara'melo]
canned food	**conservas** (f pl)	[kon'serβas]
cappuccino	**capuchino** (m)	[kapu'ʧino]
caraway	**comino** (m)	[ko'mino]
carbohydrates	**carbohidratos** (m pl)	[karβoi'ðratos]
carbonated	**gaseoso** (adj)	[gase'oso]
carp	**carpa** (f)	['karpa]
carrot	**zanahoria** (f)	[θana'orja]
catfish	**siluro** (m)	[si'lʲuro]
cauliflower	**coliflor** (f)	[koli'flor]
caviar	**caviar** (m)	[ka'βjar]
celery	**apio** (m)	['apjo]
cep	**seta calabaza** (f)	['seta kala'βaθa]
cereal crops	**cereales** (m pl)	[θere'ales]
cereal grains	**cereal molido grueso**	[θere'alʲ mo'liðo gru'eso]
champagne	**champaña** (f)	[ʧam'panja]
chanterelle	**rebozuelo** (m)	[reβoθu'elo]
check	**cuenta** (f)	[ku'enta]
cheese	**queso** (m)	['keso]
chewing gum	**chicle** (m)	['ʧikle]
chicken	**gallina** (f)	[ga'jina]
chocolate	**chocolate** (m)	[ʧoko'lʲate]
chocolate	**de chocolate** (adj)	[de ʧoko'lʲate]
cinnamon	**canela** (f)	[ka'nelʲa]
clear soup	**caldo** (m)	['kalʲðo]
cloves	**clavo** (m)	['klʲaβo]
cocktail	**cóctel** (m)	['koktelʲ]
coconut	**nuez** (f) **de coco**	[nu'eθ de 'koko]
cod	**bacalao** (m)	[baka'lʲao]
coffee	**café** (m)	[ka'fe]
coffee with milk	**café** (m) **con leche**	[ka'fe kon 'leʧe]
cognac	**coñac** (m)	[ko'njak]
cold	**frío** (adj)	['frio]
condensed milk	**leche** (f) **condensada**	['leʧe konden'saða]
condiment	**condimento** (m)	[kondi'mento]
confectionery	**pasteles** (m pl)	[pas'teles]
cookies	**galletas** (f pl)	[ga'jetas]
coriander	**cilantro** (m)	[θi'lʲantro]
corkscrew	**sacacorchos** (m)	[saka'korʧos]
corn	**maíz** (m)	[ma'iθ]
corn	**maíz** (m)	[ma'iθ]
cornflakes	**copos** (m pl) **de maíz**	['kopos de ma'iθ]
course, dish	**plato** (m)	['plʲato]
cowberry	**arándano** (m) **rojo**	[a'randano 'roχo]
crab	**cangrejo** (m) **de mar**	[kan'greχo de 'mar]
cranberry	**arándano** (m) **agrio**	[a'randano 'aɣrjo]
cream	**nata** (f) **líquida**	['nata 'likiða]
crumb	**miga** (f)	['miɣa]

crustaceans	**crustáceos** (m pl)	[krus'taθeos]
cucumber	**pepino** (m)	[pe'pino]
cuisine	**cocina** (f)	[ko'θina]
cup	**taza** (f)	['taθa]
dark beer	**cerveza** (f) **negra**	[θer'βeθa 'neɣra]
date	**dátil** (m)	['datilʲ]
death cap	**oronja** (f) **verde**	[o'ronχa 'berðe]
dessert	**postre** (m)	['postre]
diet	**dieta** (f)	[di'eta]
dill	**eneldo** (m)	[e'nelʲðo]
dinner	**cena** (f)	['θena]
dried	**seco** (adj)	['seko]
drinking water	**agua** (f) **potable**	['aɣua po'taβle]
duck	**pato** (m)	['pato]
ear	**espiga** (f)	[es'piɣa]
edible mushroom	**seta** (f) **comestible**	['seta komes'tiβle]
eel	**anguila** (f)	[an'gilʲa]
egg	**huevo** (m)	[u'eβo]
egg white	**clara** (f)	['klʲara]
egg yolk	**yema** (f)	['jema]
eggplant	**berenjena** (f)	[beren'χena]
eggs	**huevos** (m pl)	[u'eβos]
Enjoy your meal!	**¡Que aproveche!**	[ke apro'βetʃe]
fats	**grasas** (f pl)	['grasas]
fig	**higo** (m)	['iɣo]
filling	**relleno** (m)	[re'jeno]
fish	**pescado** (m)	[pes'kaðo]
flatfish	**lenguado** (m)	[lengu'aðo]
flour	**harina** (f)	[a'rina]
fly agaric	**matamoscas** (m)	[mata'moskas]
food	**comida** (f)	[ko'miða]
fork	**tenedor** (m)	[tene'ðor]
freshly squeezed juice	**zumo** (m) **fresco**	['θumo 'fresko]
fried	**frito** (adj)	['frito]
fried eggs	**huevos** (m pl) **fritos**	[u'eβos 'fritos]
frozen	**congelado** (adj)	[konχe'lʲaðo]
fruit	**fruto** (m)	['fruto]
game	**caza** (f) **menor**	['kaθa me'nor]
gammon	**jamón** (m) **fresco**	[χa'mon 'fresko]
garlic	**ajo** (m)	['aχo]
gin	**ginebra** (f)	[χi'neβra]
ginger	**jengibre** (m)	[χen'χiβre]
glass	**vaso** (m)	['baso]
glass	**copa** (f) **de vino**	['kopa de 'bino]
goose	**ganso** (m)	['ganso]
gooseberry	**grosella** (f) **espinosa**	[gro'seja espi'nosa]
grain	**grano** (m)	['grano]
grape	**uva** (f)	['uβa]
grapefruit	**pomelo** (m)	[po'melo]
green tea	**té** (m) **verde**	['te 'berðe]
greens	**verduras** (f pl)	[ber'ðuras]
halibut	**fletán** (m)	[fle'tan]

ham	**jamón** (m)	[χa'mon]
hamburger	**carne** (f) **picada**	['karne pi'kaða]
hamburger	**hamburguesa** (f)	[ambur'ɣesa]
hazelnut	**avellana** (f)	[aβe'jana]
herring	**arenque** (m)	[a'reŋke]
honey	**miel** (f)	[mjelʲ]
horseradish	**rábano** (m) **picante**	['raβano pi'kante]
hot	**caliente** (adj)	[ka'ljente]
ice	**hielo** (m)	['jelo]
ice-cream	**helado** (m)	[e'lʲaðo]
instant coffee	**café** (m) **soluble**	[ka'fe so'lʲuβle]
jam	**confitura** (f)	[koɱfi'tura]
jam	**confitura** (f)	[koɱfi'tura]
juice	**zumo** (m), **jugo** (m)	['θumo], ['χuɣo]
kidney bean	**fréjol** (m)	['freχolʲ]
kiwi	**kiwi** (m)	['kiwi]
knife	**cuchillo** (m)	[ku'ʧijo]
lamb	**carne** (f) **de carnero**	['karne de kar'nero]
lemon	**limón** (m)	[li'mon]
lemonade	**limonada** (f)	[limo'naða]
lentil	**lenteja** (f)	[len'teχa]
lettuce	**lechuga** (f)	[le'ʧuɣa]
light beer	**cerveza** (f) **rubia**	[θer'βeθa 'ruβja]
liqueur	**licor** (m)	[li'kor]
liquors	**bebidas** (f pl) **alcohólicas**	[be'βiðas alʲko'olikas]
liver	**hígado** (m)	['iɣaðo]
lunch	**almuerzo** (m)	[alʲmu'erθo]
mackerel	**caballa** (f)	[ka'βaja]
mandarin	**mandarina** (f)	[manda'rina]
mango	**mango** (m)	['mango]
margarine	**margarina** (f)	[marɣa'rina]
marmalade	**mermelada** (f)	[merme'lʲaða]
mashed potatoes	**puré** (m) **de patatas**	[pu're de pa'tatas]
mayonnaise	**mayonesa** (f)	[majo'nesa]
meat	**carne** (f)	['karne]
melon	**melón** (m)	[me'lon]
menu	**carta** (f), **menú** (m)	['karta], [me'nu]
milk	**leche** (f)	['leʧe]
milkshake	**batido** (m)	[ba'tiðo]
millet	**mijo** (m)	['miχo]
mineral water	**agua** (f) **mineral**	['aɣua mine'ralʲ]
morel	**colmenilla** (f)	[kolʲme'nija]
mushroom	**seta** (f)	['seta]
mustard	**mostaza** (f)	[mos'taθa]
non-alcoholic	**sin alcohol**	[sin alʲko'olʲ]
noodles	**tallarines** (m pl)	[taja'rines]
oats	**avena** (f)	[a'βena]
olive oil	**aceite** (m) **de oliva**	[a'θejte de o'liβa]
olives	**olivas** (f pl)	[o'liβas]
omelet	**tortilla** (f) **francesa**	[tor'tija fran'θesa]
onion	**cebolla** (f)	[θe'βoja]
orange	**naranja** (f)	[na'ranχa]

orange juice	**zumo** (m) **de naranja**	['θumo de na'ranχa]
orange-cap boletus	**boleto** (m) **castaño**	[bo'leto kas'tanjo]
oyster	**ostra** (f)	['ostra]
pâté	**paté** (m)	[pa'te]
papaya	**papaya** (m)	[pa'paja]
paprika	**páprika** (f)	['paprika]
parsley	**perejil** (m)	[pere'χilʲ]
pasta	**macarrones** (m pl)	[maka'rones]
pea	**guisante** (m)	[gi'sante]
peach	**melocotón** (m)	[meloko'ton]
peanut	**cacahuete** (m)	[kakau'ete]
pear	**pera** (f)	['pera]
peel	**piel** (f)	[pjelʲ]
perch	**perca** (f)	['perka]
pickled	**marinado** (adj)	[mari'naðo]
pie	**pastel** (m)	[pas'telʲ]
piece	**pedazo** (m)	[pe'ðaθo]
pike	**lucio** (m)	['lʲuθjo]
pike perch	**lucioperca** (m)	[lʲuθjo'perka]
pineapple	**ananás** (m)	[ana'nas]
pistachios	**pistachos** (m pl)	[pis'tatʃos]
pizza	**pizza** (f)	['pitsa]
plate	**plato** (m)	['plʲato]
plum	**ciruela** (f)	[θiru'elʲa]
poisonous mushroom	**seta** (f) **venenosa**	['seta bene'nosa]
pomegranate	**granada** (f)	[gra'naða]
pork	**carne** (f) **de cerdo**	['karne de 'θerðo]
porridge	**gachas** (f pl)	['gatʃas]
portion	**porción** (f)	[por'θjon]
potato	**patata** (f)	[pa'tata]
proteins	**proteínas** (f pl)	[prote'inas]
pub, bar	**bar** (m)	[bar]
pudding	**pudín** (f)	[pu'ðin]
pumpkin	**calabaza** (f)	[kalʲa'βaθa]
rabbit	**conejo** (m)	[ko'neχo]
radish	**rábano** (m)	['raβano]
raisin	**pasas** (f pl)	['pasas]
raspberry	**frambuesa** (f)	[frambu'esa]
recipe	**receta** (f)	[re'θeta]
red pepper	**pimienta** (f) **roja**	[pi'mjenta 'roχa]
red wine	**vino** (m) **tinto**	['bino 'tinto]
redcurrant	**grosella** (f) **roja**	[gro'seja 'roχa]
refreshing drink	**refresco** (m)	[re'fresko]
rice	**arroz** (m)	[a'roθ]
rum	**ron** (m)	[ron]
russula	**rúsula** (f)	['rusulʲa]
rye	**centeno** (m)	[θen'teno]
saffron	**azafrán** (m)	[aθa'fran]
salad	**ensalada** (f)	[ensa'lʲaða]
salmon	**salmón** (m)	[salʲ'mon]
salt	**sal** (f)	[salʲ]
salty	**salado** (adj)	[sa'lʲaðo]

sandwich	**bocadillo** (m)	[boka'ðijo]
sardine	**sardina** (f)	[sar'ðina]
sauce	**salsa** (f)	['salʲsa]
saucer	**platillo** (m)	[plʲa'tijo]
sausage	**salchichón** (m)	[salʲʧi'ʧon]
seafood	**mariscos** (m pl)	[ma'riskos]
sesame	**sésamo** (m)	['sesamo]
shark	**tiburón** (m)	[tiβu'ron]
shrimp	**camarón** (m)	[kama'ron]
side dish	**guarnición** (f)	[guarni'θjon]
slice	**loncha** (f)	['lonχa]
smoked	**ahumado** (adj)	[au'maðo]
soft drink	**bebida** (f) **sin alcohol**	[be'βiða sin alʲko'olʲ]
soup	**sopa** (f)	['sopa]
soup spoon	**cuchara** (f) **de sopa**	[ku'ʧara de 'sopa]
sour cherry	**guinda** (f)	['ginda]
sour cream	**nata** (f) **agria**	['nata 'aɣrja]
soy	**soya** (f)	['soja]
spaghetti	**espagueti** (m)	[espa'ɣeti]
sparkling	**con gas**	[kon 'gas]
spice	**especia** (f)	[es'peθja]
spinach	**espinaca** (f)	[espi'naka]
spiny lobster	**langosta** (f)	[lʲan'gosta]
spoon	**cuchara** (f)	[ku'ʧara]
squid	**calamar** (m)	[kalʲa'mar]
steak	**bistec** (m)	[bis'tek]
still	**sin gas**	[sin 'gas]
strawberry	**fresa** (f)	['fresa]
sturgeon	**esturión** (m)	[estu'rjon]
sugar	**azúcar** (m)	[a'θukar]
sunflower oil	**aceite** (m) **de girasol**	[a'θejte de χira'solʲ]
sweet	**azucarado, dulce** (adj)	[aθuka'raðo], ['dulʲθe]
sweet cherry	**cereza** (f)	[θe'reθa]
taste, flavor	**sabor** (m)	[sa'βor]
tasty	**sabroso** (adj)	[sa'βroso]
tea	**té** (m)	[te]
teaspoon	**cucharilla** (f)	[kuʧa'rija]
tip	**propina** (f)	[pro'pina]
tomato	**tomate** (m)	[to'mate]
tomato juice	**jugo** (m) **de tomate**	['χuɣo de to'mate]
tongue	**lengua** (f)	['lengua]
toothpick	**mondadientes** (m)	[monda'ðjentes]
trout	**trucha** (f)	['truʧa]
tuna	**atún** (m)	[a'tun]
turkey	**pava** (f)	['paβa]
turnip	**nabo** (m)	['naβo]
veal	**carne** (f) **de ternera**	['karne de ter'nera]
vegetable oil	**aceite** (m) **vegetal**	[a'θejte beχe'talʲ]
vegetables	**legumbres** (f pl)	[le'ɣumbres]
vegetarian	**vegetariano** (m)	[beχeta'rjano]
vegetarian	**vegetariano** (adj)	[beχeta'rjano]
vermouth	**vermú** (m)	[ber'mu]

vienna sausage	**salchicha** (f)	[salʲ'ʧiʧa]
vinegar	**vinagre** (m)	[bi'naɣre]
vitamin	**vitamina** (f)	[bita'mina]
vodka	**vodka** (m)	['boðka]
waffles	**gofre** (m)	['gofre]
waiter	**camarero** (m)	[kama'rero]
waitress	**camarera** (f)	[kama'rera]
walnut	**nuez** (f)	[nu'eθ]
water	**agua** (f)	['aɣua]
watermelon	**sandía** (f)	[san'dia]
wheat	**trigo** (m)	['triɣo]
whiskey	**whisky** (m)	['wiski]
white wine	**vino** (m) **blanco**	['bino 'blʲaŋko]
wild strawberry	**fresa** (f) **silvestre**	['fresa silʲ'βestre]
wine	**vino** (m)	['bino]
wine list	**carta** (f) **de vinos**	['karta de 'binos]
with ice	**con hielo**	[kon 'jelo]
yogurt	**yogur** (m)	[jo'ɣur]
zucchini	**calabacín** (m)	[kalʲaβa'θin]

Spanish-English gastronomic glossary

¡Que aproveche!	[ke apro'βeʧe]	Enjoy your meal!
abrebotellas (m)	[aβre·βo'tejas]	bottle opener
abrelatas (m)	[aβre·'lʲatas]	can opener
aceite (m) **de girasol**	[a'θejte de χira'solʲ]	sunflower oil
aceite (m) **de oliva**	[a'θejte de o'liβa]	olive oil
aceite (m) **vegetal**	[a'θejte beχe'talʲ]	vegetable oil
agua (f)	['aɣua]	water
agua (f) **mineral**	['aɣua mine'ralʲ]	mineral water
agua (f) **potable**	['aɣua po'taβle]	drinking water
aguacate (m)	[aɣua'kate]	avocado
ahumado (adj)	[au'maðo]	smoked
ajo (m)	['aχo]	garlic
albahaca (f)	[alʲβa'aka]	basil
albaricoque (m)	[alʲβari'koke]	apricot
alcachofa (f)	[alʲka'ʧofa]	artichoke
alforfón (m)	[alʲfor'fon]	buckwheat
almendra (f)	[alʲ'mendra]	almond
almuerzo (m)	[alʲmu'erθo]	lunch
amargo (adj)	[a'marɣo]	bitter
anís (m)	[a'nis]	anise
ananás (m)	[ana'nas]	pineapple
anguila (f)	[an'gilʲa]	eel
aperitivo (m)	[aperi'tiβo]	aperitif
apetito (m)	[ape'tito]	appetite
apio (m)	['apjo]	celery
arándano (m)	[a'randano]	bilberry
arándano (m) **agrio**	[a'randano 'aɣrjo]	cranberry
arándano (m) **rojo**	[a'randano 'roχo]	cowberry
arenque (m)	[a'reŋke]	herring
arroz (m)	[a'roθ]	rice
atún (m)	[a'tun]	tuna
avellana (f)	[aβe'jana]	hazelnut
avena (f)	[a'βena]	oats
azúcar (m)	[a'θukar]	sugar
azafrán (m)	[aθa'fran]	saffron
azucarado, dulce (adj)	[aθuka'raðo], ['dulʲθe]	sweet
bacalao (m)	[baka'lʲao]	cod
banana (f)	[ba'nana]	banana
bar (m)	[bar]	pub, bar
barman (m)	['barman]	bartender
batido (m)	[ba'tiðo]	milkshake
baya (f)	['baja]	berry
bayas (f pl)	['bajas]	berries
bebida (f) **sin alcohol**	[be'βiða sin alʲko'olʲ]	soft drink

bebidas (f pl) **alcohólicas**	[be'βiðas al^{j}ko'olikas]	liquors
beicon (m)	['bejkon]	bacon
berenjena (f)	[beren'χena]	eggplant
bistec (m)	[bis'tek]	steak
bocadillo (m)	[boka'ðijo]	sandwich
boleto (m) **áspero**	[bo'leto 'aspero]	birch bolete
boleto (m) **castaño**	[bo'leto kas'tanjo]	orange-cap boletus
brócoli (m)	['brokoli]	broccoli
brema (f)	['brema]	bream
cóctel (m)	['koktel^{j}]	cocktail
caballa (f)	[ka'βaja]	mackerel
cacahuete (m)	[kakau'ete]	peanut
café (m)	[ka'fe]	coffee
café (m) **con leche**	[ka'fe kon 'letʃe]	coffee with milk
café (m) **solo**	[ka'fe 'solo]	black coffee
café (m) **soluble**	[ka'fe so'l^{j}uβle]	instant coffee
calabacín (m)	[kal^{j}aβa'θin]	zucchini
calabaza (f)	[kal^{j}a'βaθa]	pumpkin
calamar (m)	[kal^{j}a'mar]	squid
caldo (m)	['kal^{j}ðo]	clear soup
caliente (adj)	[ka'ljente]	hot
caloría (f)	[kalo'ria]	calorie
camarón (m)	[kama'ron]	shrimp
camarera (f)	[kama'rera]	waitress
camarero (m)	[kama'rero]	waiter
canela (f)	[ka'nel^{j}a]	cinnamon
cangrejo (m) **de mar**	[kan'greχo de 'mar]	crab
capuchino (m)	[kapu'tʃino]	cappuccino
caramelo (m)	[kara'melo]	candy
carbohidratos (m pl)	[karβoi'ðratos]	carbohydrates
carne (f)	['karne]	meat
carne (f) **de carnero**	['karne de kar'nero]	lamb
carne (f) **de cerdo**	['karne de 'θerðo]	pork
carne (f) **de ternera**	['karne de ter'nera]	veal
carne (f) **de vaca**	['karne de 'baka]	beef
carne (f) **picada**	['karne pi'kaða]	hamburger
carpa (f)	['karpa]	carp
carta (f) **de vinos**	['karta de 'binos]	wine list
carta (f), **menú** (m)	['karta], [me'nu]	menu
caviar (m)	[ka'βjar]	caviar
caza (f) **menor**	['kaθa me'nor]	game
cebada (f)	[θe'βaða]	barley
cebolla (f)	[θe'βoja]	onion
cena (f)	['θena]	dinner
centeno (m)	[θen'teno]	rye
cereal molido grueso	[θere'al^{j} mo'liðo gru'eso]	cereal grains
cereales (m pl)	[θere'ales]	cereal crops
cereza (f)	[θe'reθa]	sweet cherry
cerveza (f)	[θer'βeθa]	beer
cerveza (f) **negra**	[θer'βeθa 'neɣra]	dark beer
cerveza (f) **rubia**	[θer'βeθa 'ruβja]	light beer
champaña (f)	[tʃam'panja]	champagne

chicle (m)	['ʧikle]	chewing gum
chocolate (m)	[ʧoko'lʲate]	chocolate
cilantro (m)	[θi'lʲantro]	coriander
ciruela (f)	[θiru'elʲa]	plum
clara (f)	['klʲara]	egg white
clavo (m)	['klʲaβo]	cloves
coñac (m)	[ko'njak]	cognac
cocido en agua (adj)	[ko'θiðo en 'aɣua]	boiled
cocina (f)	[ko'θina]	cuisine
col (f)	[kolʲ]	cabbage
col (f) **de Bruselas**	[kolʲ de bru'selʲas]	Brussels sprouts
coliflor (f)	[koli'flor]	cauliflower
colmenilla (f)	[kolʲme'nija]	morel
comida (f)	[ko'miða]	food
comino (m)	[ko'mino]	caraway
con gas	[kon 'gas]	sparkling
con hielo	[kon 'jelo]	with ice
condimento (m)	[kondi'mento]	condiment
conejo (m)	[ko'neχo]	rabbit
confitura (f)	[koɱfi'tura]	jam
confitura (f)	[koɱfi'tura]	jam
congelado (adj)	[konχe'lʲaðo]	frozen
conservas (f pl)	[kon'serβas]	canned food
copa (f) **de vino**	['kopa de 'bino]	glass
copos (m pl) **de maíz**	['kopos de ma'iθ]	cornflakes
crema (f) **de mantequilla**	['krema de mante'kija]	buttercream
crustáceos (m pl)	[krus'taθeos]	crustaceans
cuchara (f)	[ku'ʧara]	spoon
cuchara (f) **de sopa**	[ku'ʧara de 'sopa]	soup spoon
cucharilla (f)	[kuʧa'rija]	teaspoon
cuchillo (m)	[ku'ʧijo]	knife
cuenta (f)	[ku'enta]	check
dátil (m)	['datilʲ]	date
de chocolate (adj)	[de ʧoko'lʲate]	chocolate
desayuno (m)	[desa'juno]	breakfast
dieta (f)	[di'eta]	diet
eneldo (m)	[e'nelʲðo]	dill
ensalada (f)	[ensa'lʲaða]	salad
entremés (m)	[entre'mes]	appetizer
espárrago (m)	[es'paraɣo]	asparagus
espagueti (m)	[espa'ɣeti]	spaghetti
especia (f)	[es'peθja]	spice
espiga (f)	[es'piɣa]	ear
espinaca (f)	[espi'naka]	spinach
esturión (m)	[estu'rjon]	sturgeon
fletán (m)	[fle'tan]	halibut
fréjol (m)	['freχolʲ]	kidney bean
frío (adj)	['frio]	cold
frambuesa (f)	[frambu'esa]	raspberry
fresa (f)	['fresa]	strawberry
fresa (f) **silvestre**	['fresa silʲ'βestre]	wild strawberry
frito (adj)	['frito]	fried

fruto (m)	['fruto]	fruit
gachas (f pl)	['gatʃas]	porridge
galletas (f pl)	[ga'jetas]	cookies
gallina (f)	[ga'jina]	chicken
ganso (m)	['ganso]	goose
gaseoso (adj)	[gase'oso]	carbonated
ginebra (f)	[χi'neβra]	gin
gofre (m)	['gofre]	waffles
granada (f)	[gra'naða]	pomegranate
grano (m)	['grano]	grain
grasas (f pl)	['grasas]	fats
grosella (f) **espinosa**	[gro'seja espi'nosa]	gooseberry
grosella (f) **negra**	[gro'seja 'neɣra]	blackcurrant
grosella (f) **roja**	[gro'seja 'roχa]	redcurrant
guarnición (f)	[guarni'θjon]	side dish
guinda (f)	['ginda]	sour cherry
guisante (m)	[gi'sante]	pea
hígado (m)	['iɣaðo]	liver
habas (f pl)	['aβas]	beans
hamburguesa (f)	[ambur'ɣesa]	hamburger
harina (f)	[a'rina]	flour
helado (m)	[e'lʲaðo]	ice-cream
hielo (m)	['jelo]	ice
higo (m)	['iɣo]	fig
hoja (f) **de laurel**	['oχa de lʲau'relʲ]	bay leaf
huevo (m)	[u'eβo]	egg
huevos (m pl)	[u'eβos]	eggs
huevos (m pl) **fritos**	[u'eβos 'fritos]	fried eggs
jamón (m)	[χa'mon]	ham
jamón (m) **fresco**	[χa'mon 'fresko]	gammon
jengibre (m)	[χen'χiβre]	ginger
jugo (m) **de tomate**	['χuɣo de to'mate]	tomato juice
kiwi (m)	['kiwi]	kiwi
langosta (f)	[lʲan'gosta]	spiny lobster
leche (f)	['letʃe]	milk
leche (f) **condensada**	['letʃe konden'saða]	condensed milk
lechuga (f)	[le'tʃuɣa]	lettuce
legumbres (f pl)	[le'ɣumbres]	vegetables
lengua (f)	['lengua]	tongue
lenguado (m)	[lengu'aðo]	flatfish
lenteja (f)	[len'teχa]	lentil
licor (m)	[li'kor]	liqueur
limón (m)	[li'mon]	lemon
limonada (f)	[limo'naða]	lemonade
loncha (f)	['lonχa]	slice
lucio (m)	['lʲuθjo]	pike
lucioperca (m)	[lʲuθjo'perka]	pike perch
maíz (m)	[ma'iθ]	corn
maíz (m)	[ma'iθ]	corn
macarrones (m pl)	[maka'rones]	pasta
mandarina (f)	[manda'rina]	mandarin
mango (m)	['mango]	mango

mantequilla (f)	[mante'kija]	butter
manzana (f)	[man'θana]	apple
margarina (f)	[marɣa'rina]	margarine
marinado (adj)	[mari'naðo]	pickled
mariscos (m pl)	[ma'riskos]	seafood
matamoscas (m)	[mata'moskas]	fly agaric
mayonesa (f)	[majo'nesa]	mayonnaise
melón (m)	[me'lon]	melon
melocotón (m)	[meloko'ton]	peach
mermelada (f)	[merme'lʲaða]	marmalade
miel (f)	[mjelʲ]	honey
miga (f)	['miɣa]	crumb
mijo (m)	['miχo]	millet
mondadientes (m)	[monda'ðjentes]	toothpick
mostaza (f)	[mos'taθa]	mustard
nabo (m)	['naβo]	turnip
naranja (f)	[na'ranχa]	orange
nata (f) **agria**	['nata 'aɣrja]	sour cream
nata (f) **líquida**	['nata 'likiða]	cream
nuez (f)	[nu'eθ]	walnut
nuez (f) **de coco**	[nu'eθ de 'koko]	coconut
olivas (f pl)	[o'liβas]	olives
oronja (f) **verde**	[o'ronχa 'berðe]	death cap
ostra (f)	['ostra]	oyster
páprika (f)	['paprika]	paprika
pan (m)	[pan]	bread
papaya (m)	[pa'paja]	papaya
pasas (f pl)	['pasas]	raisin
pastel (m)	[pas'telʲ]	pie
pasteles (m pl)	[pas'teles]	confectionery
paté (m)	[pa'te]	pâté
patata (f)	[pa'tata]	potato
pato (m)	['pato]	duck
pava (f)	['paβa]	turkey
pedazo (m)	[pe'ðaθo]	piece
pepino (m)	[pe'pino]	cucumber
pera (f)	['pera]	pear
perca (f)	['perka]	perch
perejil (m)	[pere'χilʲ]	parsley
pescado (m)	[pes'kaðo]	fish
piel (f)	[pjelʲ]	peel
pimentón (m)	[pimen'ton]	bell pepper
pimienta (f) **negra**	[pi'mjenta 'neɣra]	black pepper
pimienta (f) **roja**	[pi'mjenta 'roχa]	red pepper
pistachos (m pl)	[pis'tatʃos]	pistachios
pizza (f)	['pitsa]	pizza
platillo (m)	[plʲa'tijo]	saucer
plato (m)	['plʲato]	course, dish
plato (m)	['plʲato]	plate
pomelo (m)	[po'melo]	grapefruit
porción (f)	[por'θjon]	portion
postre (m)	['postre]	dessert

propina (f) [pro'pina] tip
proteínas (f pl) [prote'inas] proteins
pudín (f) [pu'ðin] pudding
puré (m) **de patatas** [pu're de pa'tatas] mashed potatoes
queso (m) ['keso] cheese
rábano (m) ['raβano] radish
rábano (m) **picante** ['raβano pi'kante] horseradish
rúsula (f) ['rusulʲa] russula
rebozuelo (m) [reβoθu'elo] chanterelle
receta (f) [re'θeta] recipe
refresco (m) [re'fresko] refreshing drink
regusto (m) [re'ɣusto] aftertaste
relleno (m) [re'jeno] filling
remolacha (f) [remo'lʲatʃa] beetroot
ron (m) [ron] rum
sésamo (m) ['sesamo] sesame
sabor (m) [sa'βor] taste, flavor
sabroso (adj) [sa'βroso] tasty
sacacorchos (m) [saka'kortʃos] corkscrew
sal (f) [salʲ] salt
salado (adj) [sa'lʲaðo] salty
salchichón (m) [salʲtʃi'tʃon] sausage
salchicha (f) [salʲ'tʃitʃa] vienna sausage
salmón (m) [salʲ'mon] salmon
salmón (m) **del Atlántico** [salʲ'mon delʲ at'lʲantiko] Atlantic salmon
salsa (f) ['salʲsa] sauce
sandía (f) [san'dia] watermelon
sardina (f) [sar'ðina] sardine
seco (adj) ['seko] dried
seta (f) ['seta] mushroom
seta (f) **comestible** ['seta komes'tiβle] edible mushroom
seta (f) **venenosa** ['seta bene'nosa] poisonous mushroom
seta calabaza (f) ['seta kala'βaθa] cep
siluro (m) [si'lʲuro] catfish
sin alcohol [sin alʲko'olʲ] non-alcoholic
sin gas [sin 'gas] still
sopa (f) ['sopa] soup
soya (f) ['soja] soy
té (m) [te] tea
té (m) **negro** ['te 'neɣro] black tea
té (m) **verde** ['te 'berðe] green tea
tallarines (m pl) [taja'rines] noodles
tarta (f) ['tarta] cake
tarta (f) ['tarta] cake
taza (f) ['taθa] cup
tenedor (m) [tene'ðor] fork
tiburón (m) [tiβu'ron] shark
tomate (m) [to'mate] tomato
tortilla (f) **francesa** [tor'tija fran'θesa] omelet
trigo (m) ['triɣo] wheat
trucha (f) ['trutʃa] trout
uva (f) ['uβa] grape

vaso (m)	['baso]	glass
vegetariano (adj)	[beχeta'rjano]	vegetarian
vegetariano (m)	[beχeta'rjano]	vegetarian
verduras (f pl)	[ber'ðuras]	greens
vermú (m)	[ber'mu]	vermouth
vinagre (m)	[bi'naɣre]	vinegar
vino (m)	['bino]	wine
vino (m) **blanco**	['bino 'blʲaŋko]	white wine
vino (m) **tinto**	['bino 'tinto]	red wine
vitamina (f)	[bita'mina]	vitamin
vodka (m)	['boðka]	vodka
whisky (m)	['wiski]	whiskey
yema (f)	['jema]	egg yolk
yogur (m)	[jo'ɣur]	yogurt
zanahoria (f)	[θana'orja]	carrot
zarzamoras (f pl)	[θarθa'moras]	blackberry
zumo (m) **de naranja**	['θumo de na'ranχa]	orange juice
zumo (m) **fresco**	['θumo 'fresko]	freshly squeezed juice
zumo (m), **jugo** (m)	['θumo], ['χuɣo]	juice

www.ingramcontent.com/pod-product-compliance
Lightning Source LLC
LaVergne TN
LVHW051731080426
835511LV00018B/3001

* 9 7 8 1 7 8 4 9 2 4 5 0 8 *